Children's Sweaters and Hats

Knitting Seamless Raglan Top Down

Crayon Pullover

Strawberry Twist

Rapunzel

Circumnavigate

Children's Sweaters and Hats

Knitting Seamless Raglan Top Down

Ripples Knit's Kin

Plain and Simple

Mary Rich Goodwin

Children's Sweaters and Hats–Knitting Seamless Raglan Top Down
Step by Step Patterns and Photos
by Mary Rich Goodwin

Acknowledgments

Thank goodness for good knitting friends who are willing to lend an editing hand. A big thanks goes to Ted and Cynthia Schofield, Elizabeth J. Smith, Allyson Wray, Erin Christensen, Karla Wonacott and everyone else at Heindselman's Knit Shop who helped edit these patterns. Another thanks goes to my dear husband who unquestionably loves and accepts me and my crazy knitting whenever and wherever we go. Last, thanks to my six children who so patiently waited for mom, dinner, and the laundry while she worked on these two books.

Publisher's Cataloging-in-Publication
(Provided by Quality Books, Inc.)

Goodwin, Mary Rich.
    Children's Sweaters & hats–knitting seamless
raglan top down : step by step patterns & photos /
Mary Goodwin. -- 1st ed.
    p. cm.
    LCCN: 00-102563
    ISBN: 1-88810-652-2

    1. Knitting--Patterns. 2. Sweaters. 3. Hats.
4. Children's clothing. I. Title

TT825.G66 2000   746.43'20432
                        QBI00-444

Also available
Adult Sweaters–Knitting Seamless Raglan Top Down
Step by Step Patterns and Photos
ISBN 1888106541 (Adult) $14.95
Available from your book or craft store, or by calling Agreka Books.

Cover photographs Mary Rich Goodwin
Cover design Lea Taylor

Agreka Books
800 360-5284
www.agreka.com

Table of Contents

Introduction   2

Notes on Patterns   3
    Abbreviations   3
    Yarn   4
    Yardage Chart   5
    Yarn Gauge   5
    Needle Conversion   5
    Gauge   6
    Needles   6
    Casting On   7
    Increase Stitch   7
    Adding Colors   8
    Stripeless Stripe   8
    Markers   8
    Sizing   9
    Ribbing   9
    Short Rows   9
    Button bands   11
    Binding off   11
    Blocking   11

1. Homespun   12
Cardigan knit with soft bulky yarn, simple and warm.

2. Ring Around the Cardigan   16
Rolled edge with a checkered ring around the neck in contrasting colors.

3. ZigZag   20
Two colors knit alternatively in the yoke and cuffs, mix to make this pullover fun.

4. Wacky Waves   25
Bright stripes on a dark background with increases and decreases for wave appearance.

5. Little Fair Isle Hood   28
Fair isle band through the front of this pullover, topped with a hood.

6. Bright Heart   32
Sweater and matching hat with bright motifs on a dark background sweater.

7. Crayon   37
Bright bold elongated colors intermixed in the yoke of this pullover.

8. Circumnavigate   43
A solid knit pullover with a fair isle band through the middle of the body and sleeves.

9. YumYum Greens   47
A base of a tan sweater topped with different shades of green and yellow for a bright and cheery sweater.

10. Rapunzel   52
A solid colored pullover with cables flowing from the neck down, embroidered with small flowers on the front.

11. Strawberry Twist   55
A solid colored pullover, knit with twists and yarn overs for a textured sweater

Design Challenge   59

Yarn Sources   60

Stitch Glossary   61

Index   63

Introduction

In 1998, I compiled my favorite patterns into a book RichDesigns One Piece Knitting, which I sold over the Internet and through craft stores. It was a success.

Now I have created eleven patterns for each of my two new books

Children Seamless Sweaters & Hats Knitting Seamless Raglan Top Down
Step by Step Patterns & Photos
Adult Sweaters Knitting Seamless Raglan Top Down
Step by Step Patterns & Photos

Of the over 2000 sweaters I have designed and knit, people say they love these beautiful sweaters the best. This book contains seamless patterns knit from the top down. With circular and double point needles, the seamless sweater is accomplished. The increases are hidden in the yoke of the sweater by working a Make 1 stitch. The texture of the yarn is important since it also helps hide the increase stitches. I call these raglan-less sweaters since there are no noticeable raglan lines down the yoke. Once the yoke is complete, the sleeves are knit circular all the way down to the cuff, using either shorter circular needles, or DP needles. The body is then knit circular on longer circular needles and there are no seams to knit together.

I explain various techniques and the reason and explanation for the different needles. I also provide helpful tips, a stitch glossary, and a design section with ideas for designing your own motifs, plus a sample of knitting graph paper for you to use.

The patterns I enjoy knitting the most are the top down seamless raglan, which I worked and changed until I had the proportions just right. It is like magic cast on so many, work the neck ribbing, divide for sleeves, front and back, and viola, a sweater. The pattern seemed to work for any size sweater knit the yoke longer and the sweater is larger.

Once you have the process down, I encourage you to use the basic sweater and try designing for yourself. Branch out and change colors, designs, add stripes or textures and create your own original sweater.

After four years teaching in the classroom, I went back to school to obtain two masters degrees in education. I began to understand even more clearly what it takes to be an effective teacher on any topic. After I published my first book, I began to learn more about writing patterns for others. Through a vast audience of knitters worldwide, I've received feedback and suggestions.

Knitting sweaters is easy for me, writing the instructions is the challenge. I've checked and re-checked these patterns, and had other knitters check and test knit them. My goal is for each pattern to be versatile enough for the knitter to pick and choose parts of the patterns and individualize them to their liking. If you come across problems, or need clarification, please contact me through email or regular mail and I will respond.

Mary Rich Goodwin
660 South 1550 East
Pleasant Grove, UT 84062
mgoodwin@utah.uswest.net

Notes on Patterns

These patterns could be referred to as "Variations on a Theme." Many of the techniques used in this book allow the patterns to be knit seamless. The goal was to make each pattern user friendly with all the information needed included with that pattern. Incorporated in these notes are some hints and tricks for making parts of knitting these sweaters easier and more professional looking. There are a few things used in most of the patterns that will be explained here and in the pattern. They are listed in the order you would need them for a knitting project, not alphabetically.

Abbreviations listed alphabetically
For more complete instructions, see stitch glossary

" --- inches
beg ---beginning
bm---beginning marker
bo----bind off
cc---contrast color
circ---circular
cn---cable needle
co--- cast on
dec---decrease
dk---double knitting weight
dp---double point needles
inc---increased
k---knit
k1inc---Knit 1 increase
k2tog---knit 2 sts together
k3tog---knit 3 sts together
lt tw---left twist
M1---Make one stitch
mc---main color
meas---measures
ndl---needle
p----purl
patt---pattern

pm---place marker
psso---pass slipped st over
rem---remaining
rep---repeat
rh---right hand
rnd---round
rs---right side
rt tw---right twist
sk---skip
sl----slip
ssk---slip, slip, knit
sm---slip marker
St st---stockinette stitch
tbl---through back loop
ws---wrong side
yb--- yarn back-
yds---yards
yf---yarn forward
yo---yarn over
4 st rt cable---4 stitch right cable
4 st lt cable---4 stitch left cable
6 st rt cable---6 stitch right cable
6 st rt cable---6 stitch left cable

Yarn

Texture

The following qualities of yarn work great these sweaters; textured yarn such as tweeds, multi-color, multi-strand yarns, boucle, or nubby yarns work well. There isn't one particular kind that must be used, instead, find a yarn you like and with its imperfect color or texture, you are set to knit.

Weight

You have the freedom to choose the weight of yarn you like with just about any of these patterns. If you like a thinner weight, choose a dk (double knit), or sport weight yarn. Smaller needles such as a size 6 or smaller may need to be used with the thinner yarn. The same applies to a bulky yarn, a larger size 10 or 10 1/2 needle may be a better size for that yarn. The determining factor for these patterns is the length of the yoke. The longer you knit the yoke, the larger the sweater size. As long as you make the neck large enough, the yoke determines the size of the sweater. Knit a swatch to determine gauge and looseness of desired stitch.

Fiber Content

Knit with fibers you like. Choose wool, acrylic, cotton, blends, mix and match. Make sure the washing instructions are the same for all the yarns used. If they are all machine washable, they are interchangeable. If they have different fiber and some are washable, while others are dry clean only, you may have problems. Treat all the fibers like the most delicate one you are using. If using a non-mercerized cotton, be aware the sweater will shrink, allow for this.

Colors

Have fun with colors, mix and match, use up what you have, or buy what you want. Many of these patterns can be knit for either male or female. Change the colors to suit your individual preference. Can't decided what colors to use, look to nature for your answer. Find a picture or place you find beautiful, look at the colors that are found there and match them to yarns. Many of these sweaters were designed during the fall, consequently, fall colors show in my selection.

Amount

Each variety of yarn will contain different yardage. Grams or ounces alone can vary with yardage. Check the chart included in these notes to find the yardage needed for the size sweater to be knit and the weight of yarn to be used. Each pattern will also include total yardage needed to knit the garment. Make sure you buy enough yarn to complete your project. Nothing is more disappointing than to almost finish a sweater and run out of yarn, only to find you can't match it again.

How Much Yarn Do I Need? Yardage given for sizes toddler 2 to XXXL using Stockinette Stitch. Aran knits may use 1/3 more yardage.

Size	Chest	Bulky Yarn	Worsted Weight	Sport Weight
Toddler 2	22"	350 yds	420 yds	500 yds
Toddler 4	24"	400 yds	500 yds	600 yds
Size 5-6	26"	500 yds	600 yds	700 yds
Size 8-10	28"	650 yds	800 yds	950 yds
Size 12-14	30"	800 yds	950 yds	1100 yds
Small	32 to 34"	900 yds	1050 yds	1300 yds
Medium	36 to 38"	1000 yds	1150 yds	1400 yds
Large	40 to 42"	1100 yds	1250 yds	1600 yds
X-Large	44 to 46"	1200 yds	1450 yds	1800 yds
XX-Large	48 to 50"	1400 yds	1700 yds	2000 yds
XXX-Large	52 to 54"	1600 yds	1950 yds	2200 yds

Standard Weight Yarn Gauge

Bulky	3 1/2 sts = 1 inch	4 rows = 1 inch	Size 11 needles
Worsted	5 sts = 1 inch	7 rows = 1 inch	Size 8 needles
Sport/dk	6 sts = 1 inch	8 rows = 1 inch	Size 5 needles

Needle Conversion Chart

US	Metric
1	2.25
2	2.5
3	3
4	3.5
5	3.75
6	4
7	4.5
8	5
9	5.5
10	6
10 1/2	6.5, 7, 7.5
11	8
13	9

Gauge

Choose your yarn and needles you will be using and cast on the number of stitches you need to knit 4". If the gauge is 5 sts per inch, cast on 20 sts. Knit several rows and your piece should measure 4". If it is too large, try smaller needles, if it is too small, try larger needles. Be careful not to stretch out the sample as you measure it. You might want to purl a row to separate the different sizes of needles when you change to get the correct gauge. As a general rule, 1/2 stitch difference = 1 size. In other words, if you are supposed to get 5 sts per inch and you get 4 sts per inch, and you wanted to knit a size 34, you will end up with a size 38 since the difference is 1 stitch, since 1/2 st difference = 1 size, so 1 whole stitch = 2 sizes.

You might get your sts per inch to match but find your rows don't measure up. The sts per inch are more important than the rows since the size is determined by the length of the yoke.

Needles and Other Useful Information

Circular and double point needles are the secret to knitting this sweater completely seamless. The ribbing for these sweaters is always knit on a smaller size 16" length circular needle. I like to use a size 3 needle with the sport and dk weight yarns since it produces a nice tight ribbing. A larger size 4 can be used with the worsted weight yarn and a size 6 with the bulky weight yarns. Use what you are comfortable with, or what gives you the correct gauge.

Explanation of Needle Use

All sizes use the smaller 16" circular needles for the neck, sleeve and bottom cuff ribbing.

For 3 smaller sizes 1-2-4 It's easier to use the 16" circular needles for yoke and body. The sleeves and cuffs can be worked on dp needles.

For 3 larger sizes 6-8-10 16" circular needles are used on the yoke and 24" are exchanged after yoke sts are added. The 16" needles will be used to knit the sleeves circular leaving all other sts on longer circular needle. Double point needles can also be used for seamless sleeves.

	Bulky	Worsted	Sport
Ribbing	size 6 needle	size 3`to 5 needle	size 3 needle
Body	size 10 to 10 1/2	size 8 needle	size 6 needle

If knitting a small child's sweater, it's easier to use the smaller size 16" circular needles for the neck, yoke and body. The sleeves and cuffs can be worked on dp needles since the 16" circular needles won't stretch around the sleeves.

For larger sized sweaters, the 16" circular needles are used on the ribbing and the first several inches of the yoke. Change to the larger 24" circular needles to continue the yoke and they will also be used on the body of the sweater. The 16" needles will be used to knit the sleeves circular leaving all other sts on 24" circular needles. Double point needles, the same size as the circular needles can also be utilized for seamless sleeves.

If You Don't Have all the Size Needles You Need

Don't worry, use stitch holders to hold the sts from the body and other sleeves while you knit each sleeve circular. If you can only have one length of circular needle, use the 16" length, it's easier to scrunch sts than to stretch them.

Reading Patterns

When you follow a pattern, always read between the punctuation. Read from comma to comma, comma to period, or period to period and do what it says within that section before going on to the next. When there are parenthesis, follow the instructions within them and usually what follows will tell you how many times to follow the instructions in parenthesis.

Stickies

Stickies or Post-its are a great way to keep your place in a pattern, just stick it on where you are and move it as you progress, when the sticky is gone, get another one. It is easier than getting lost and having to rip out your knitting.

Casting On

There are many different ways to cast on for the beginning of the neck ribbing. Make sure the cast on is loose enough for the opening to stretch and pull the sweater over the head comfortably.
Thumb wrap cast on: Wrap yarn around thumb from front to back and slip needle through loop from bottom to top, for a very loose cast on. The first row to knit is a little difficult, but is easier after the first row is worked. If you have another way to cast on, use it. The cast on can be fancy or plain depending on the desired look of the edge. If you are casting on and need a tail for part of the cast on, make sure you have at least 3 times the length of tail that you will need for the length you are casting on.

Increase Stitch
The Make one stitch

(M1) is one way to increase a stitch very unnoticeably. Place the left needle under the bar between the stitch just knit and the next one ready to be knit. Lift up the bar and place the right needle through the back of that bar. Wrap it like you would to knit and follow through with a knit stitch. See following diagram for picture instructions.

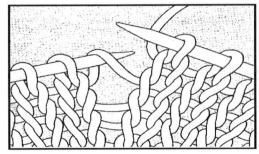 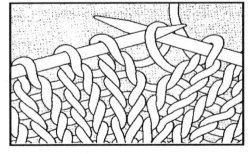

7

Scattering the M1's

When working the M1's, change their placement on each increase row so they don't line up. You can follow a pattern for placing them, or make them randomly and farther from the markers as more sts are added. Try to place them consistently the same number of sts from the marker for that same row. If you choose to place them 4 sts before and after the marker, work them 4 sts before and after the rest of the markers for that row.

M1's and a Fair Isle Pattern

If there is a motif such as a heart, place the M1 between the motifs so they aren't altered by the added sts. If you are designing your own pattern, place increases where they won't be noticed.

Raglanless to Raglan

If the M1 sts make you a little unsure, you can convert many of these patterns to a raglan by working a knit 1increase in the stitch before and the stitch after each marker, every other row. Knit 1increase (K1inc) is worked by knitting into the front of the stitch and in the back of the same stitch before slipping the stitch off the needle. The only difference will be a raglan line. This technique would not be suggested for the textured patterns or those with waves.

Adding Colors

When adding or changing colors, add the next color of yarn by placing at least a 6" tail of the yarn to be added behind the knitting, hold the new strand as if it were tied on. Secure it after 1 or 2 more rows are worked so it can be adjusted and tied with no extra slack for a flawless front.

Stripeless Stripe

To knit a different color colored stripe into your sweater, there is a trick to making it a true stripe and not one with a step in it. Lay the tail of the new yarn behind the work and hold it and knit regularly without tieing it on. Tie it when you come around to that place on the next row or even after a couple of rows. When you knit around to the place where you started the next color, knit to the stitch right before the one where you added the new color. Place the right needle in the stitch below the one you would normally knit and knit it as a regular stitch.

Markers

You can purchase commercial markers, use paper clips, or rubber bands. I like to use a contrasting color of yarn for 3 of the markers and a different color for the beginning marker. Cut a 4" length of yarn and tie it in a slip knot. For the beginning marker, wrap the marker twice on the increase rows to indicate an increase row. Place beginning marker without a double wrap on regular, non increase rows. The beginning marker is usually the marker at the beginning of the sleeve section, the next marker is the beginning of the back section and the 3rd marker is the beginning of the second sleeve. If you are using commercial markers, you can also place 2 markers together at the beginning to mark this part of the garment.

Sizing

For a really good fit, find a sweater that is the size you want to knit. Measure the yoke diagonally as if it had a raglan sleeve, that measurement is a good indicator of how long you should knit the yoke for your sweater.

Note Since yarn may vary, gauge will also vary. After checking your gauge and figuring out your size, remember the length of the yoke determines the size of the sweater. Measure it from the needle to the beginning of the ribbing from a front marker, ribbing not included in the measurement. Since short rows may be worked on the back, make sure you measure it on the front side of the sweater. This measurement is the one from the base of the neck ribbing to the underarm, measured on the front section of sweater. Larger sweaters can also be made by increasing the length of the yoke from the neck to the sleeve inseam. The longer the yoke, the larger the sweater. The proportions for the front, back and sleeves will also increase to the larger size desired. 1 inch equals about 3 more inches added to chest measurement.

Ribbing

Ribbing can be changed to suit individual likings.

*K1, p1: Work continuously over an even number of sts lining up the knit sts and purl sts.

*K2, p2: Work continuously over a multiples of 4 sts. Line up the k2's and the p 2's.

*K3, p2: Worked on multiples of 5 sts. Line up the knit and purl sts.

*Rolled edge: Knit at least 6 to 8 rows of stockinette st, then work one of the previous ribbings for 1 to 2" to help pull in the neck ribbing before working the yoke. The stockinette stitch edge will roll.

Short Rows

Short rows will add 4 extra rows on the back and part of the sleeve section of the sweater for a more comfortable fit with the back of the sweater slightly longer at the neck edge. Short rows are optional on any of the patterns and can be included only if the knitter wants to add them. The short row begins on the right side of the sweater from the beginning marker.

Short Row Explanation

Two optional short rows may be knit after neck ribbing. When working short rows, 1st row will be worked from beginning marker which is the first marker of the sleeve section, across the sleeve, across the back section and other sleeve. 2nd short row is worked right after the 1st short row 2 sts beyond on both sides of the first short row.

Short Rows Directions

Slip beginning marker, knit to the fourth marker counting the beginning marker. Knit 2 more sts, yf (yarn forward), sl 1, yb (yarn back), turn work to WS (wrong side), sl 1, purl to beginning marker, purl 2 sts past beginning marker, yb, sl 1, yf, turn work, right side, sl 1, knit to where last turn was made 2 sts past the 4th marker. Knit 2 sts past this last short row turn, yf, sl 1, yb, turn work, sl 1, purl to beginning marker, purl 4 sts beyond beginning marker. Yb, sl 1, yf, turn work, sl 1, knit to beginning marker. You have just added 4 rows to the back section of the sweater for a more comfortable fit. Each pattern will take you through the short rows step by step. Remember, the short rows are optional and will not affect the overall look of the sweater.

Knitting Sleeves Flat Instead of Circular

Any of these patterns can be knit with flat sleeves instead of circular. You may not like to use double point needles, or maybe you don't know how. You will still knit over the sleeve section and leave all other sts on longer circular needles. RS, work over sleeve sts to second marker, turn work to WS, and purl back on the back side to the beg marker. Work back and forth over sleeve sts and work the decrease every 6th row except don't work the decrease on the edge of the sleeve. Work the decreases 2 or 3 sts from the edge, which will leave you a nice edge to stitch up later. For small sweaters, you can actually knit the sleeves on dp needles, only use them like straight needles. Place a rubber band or tip protector around one of the edges, so sts don't slip off. When you have finished the sleeve and cuff, leave about an 18" tail to stitch up seam when sweater is complete.

Sleeve Decrease

The instructions for these patterns calls for two k2togs one on each side of marker to decrease sleeve inseam. With the textured yarn, this decrease is fine for both sides of the marker since decreases are unnoticeable. If you would like to have the sts both slant into the marker, work a ssk on the right side of the marker.

Under Arm Gap

After sleeves are finished ready to be worked with the body, there will be a small gap under each arm. This can be easily knit shut on the first round when joining the front and back. As you work to the underarm, slip the left needle through a stitch from the sleeve and wrap it and knit it as normal. Pick up 1 to 2 more sts to completely close this opening. On the next round of the body, where the sts were added under each arm, work 2 k2 tog's to decrease the sts added on the previous row. The gap under the arm can always be stitched up with a tapestry needle and yarn after sweater is finished

Buttonholes

Buttonholes can be worked many different ways. The method used in these patterns is to bind off 2 to 3 sts on the button band, on the next row, cast on 2 to 3 sts where the previous sts were bound off. Buttonholes should be worked 3 or more sts from the outside edge.

Button Band

The button band can be knit with the rest of the sweater, or picked up after the sweater is knit and added later. To knit on the button band, here are two ways you can work it.

1. Garter Stitch Band

This is the band worked on the patterns in this book. Work a garter stitch button band on both edges of the cardigan. Knit the first 5 sts on both the knit and purl sides of fronts while knitting sweater.

2. Ribbing Edge

After working the neck ribbing, continue working the ribbing stitch down the front 6 to 8 sts on both edges of the sweater and working button holes periodically down the buttonhole edge. Make sure you work this ribbing edge tight, it has a tendancy to be loose.

Pullover to Cardigan

If a pullover is converted to a cardigan, 4 to 6 sts need to be added to front section of sweater to compensate for the button band overlap. Divide them equally between the two front sections

Length

As styles change, so do the length of sweaters, both body and sleeves. You can adjust the length of any of these patterns to suit individual body's or fashions. Patterns can be lengthened or shortened, just work ribbing and bind off when desired length is knit. One advantage to knitting the top down sweater, the length can be changed easily without ripping out the whole sweater.

Binding Off

Make sure you bind off **loosely**. To help keep stitches loose, change the right needle to a larger size, 2 to 6 sizes larger to help keep bind off stitches loose. Double point needles also work well for the bind off.

Picot Edge Bind Off

For a variation on the regular bind off, try the following. Instead of wrapping the yarn over the top of the front and back when working the knit and purl stitch, use a double point needle for the right side and wrap yarn under work for the knit and purl stitch. Purl the knit sts and knit the purl sts while binding off and wrapping the yarn down under instead of over the top.

Blocking

After sweater is completed and hand work is done, lay garment flat on a table or counter and shape. Spray thoroughly with spray bottle and water until sweater is completely damp. Press each part of the garment, both front and back firmly with palms. Pounding with a flat hand may also help in pressing and shaping the sweater. Shape as desired and let dry. You may pin, or lay something with weight on edges to help hold the shape. Don't use heat or an iron on acrylic as the fibers can actually melt with heat.

Homespun
&
Soft
Soft as a Bunny Tail

Knit this cardigan top down, quickly with chunky weight yarn, seamless and easily. Large size 10 needles will help knit this fast. This sweater is almost like a jacket or change yarn to worsted or dk weight and adjust to smaller needles suitable for that weight yarn.

Sizes
Sweater is written for child's sizes: **2, 4, 6, 8, 10, 12.** Instructions are written for smallest size with larger sizes in parenthesis.

Sweater pictured knit with Lion Brand Homespun Tudor

Finished Chest Measurements
Chest: 24 (27, 30, 33, 36, 39)"

Materials
Yarn Chunky or Boucle' type yarn.
Total yardage needed 420 (500, 600, 700, 800, 950) yds.
Circular Needles One pair each size 4 and 10 16" length (24" length of each if possible)
Double Point Needles Size 4 and 10
Markers
Tapestry Needle

Gauge

3 to 4 sts and 4 rows = 1" knit with size 10 needles and chunky yarn in Stockinette stitch. Gauge will vary with texture of yarn.

Note Sweater is knit from the top down on smaller circular needles and as yoke stitches increase, longer circular needles are used. Shorter needles will then be used to knit sleeves circular while all other stitches remain on longer needles. For smaller sizes or if stitches become too tight, dp needles can be used for remaining sleeve and cuff.

Neck Ribbing

With size 4 circular needles cast on 72 (76, 80, 84, 88, 92) sts. Turn.

Row 1: K1, p1; rep across row. Turn.

Rep row 1; 3 more times.

Buttonhole Girls button hole should be on the right button band and boys are on the left band. On buttonhole edge of sweater, work first 3 sts, bind off next 2 sts, work across row as established. On next row, cast on 2 sts where the previous 2 were bound off. Work 3 or 4 more rows of ribbing to end wrong side (WS), wrong side is the last row worked. Change to larger size 10 needles and work preparatory row. Continue to work buttonholes evenly down button band every 3" or as often as desired.

Preparatory Row Knit 5 sts at beginning of row. K8 (9, 9, 10, 11,12), place marker, k12 (13, 14, 15, 16, 17), place marker, k 22 (22, 24, 24, 24, 25), place marker, k12 (13, 14, 15, 16, 17), place marker, k8 (9, 9, 10, 11, 11). Knit last 5 sts, turn.

Preparatory Row 2: K5, p to last 5 sts, k5, turn.

Optional short row explanation and directions (If you don't want to work short rows, begin with yoke directions) Make sure you are purling on the wrong side of work and knitting on right side. 4 optional short rows may be added to the back and part of the sleeve sections of sweater for a more comfortable fit. Directions are explained here and begin after neck ribbing is finished and you have changed to larger needles and worked preparatory rows. (WS) Slip beg marker (1st marker) and purl to the 4th marker. P2 sts past 4th marker, yarn back (yb), slip 1, yarn forward (yf), turn work to RS, slip 1 st, knit to beg marker, knit 2 sts past beginning marker, yf, sl 1 yb, turn work, WS, sl 1st, purl to where last turn was made (2 sts past the 4th marker) purl 2 more sts, yb, sl 1 st, yf, turn work, RS, sl 1 st, knit to beg marker, knit 2 sts past beg marker, yf, sl 1 yb, turn work, WS, sl 1 st, purl to end of row. Begin with yoke directions row 1.

How to Make1 stitch (M1) On knit side, with left needles, pick up the horizontal strand between last st and next st to be knit. Pick it up from front to back and knit into the back of this strand with the right needle. Strand is twisted to avoid a hole. See notes at beginning of book.

Yoke

Row 1 and all odd rows: K5, purl row to last 5 sts, k 5, turn.
Row 2: Knit row working a M1 2 sts before and after markers. (8 sts added)
Row 4: Knit row working a M1 6 sts before and after markers. (8 sts added)
Row 6: Rep row 4 working M1 4 sts before and after markers. (8 sts added)
When working the M1's, you can place them farther away from markers as more sts are added. Make sure you don't line them up, this will avoid a raglan line. Continue with this pattern of increases every even row of yoke by M1 in altering places before and after markers and continue to work buttonholes down button band until yoke measures 6 (7, 8, 9, 10, 11)" not including neck ribbing.

Sleeves

(RS) Work sts over to sleeve section which will be the stitches between the beg marker and the 2nd marker, change to shorter size 10 16" circular needles or size 10 dp needles.
Row 1: With 10 needles, knit over sleeve sts and join them to knit the sleeve circular. Place marker where sleeve joins at inseam.
Rows 2 to 5: Knit rows circular.
Row 6: Decrease 1 st before and after marker by k2tog at beg and end of 6th row.
Continue to decrease 1 st before and after the inseam marker every 6th row by k2tog until sleeve measures 6 (7, 9, 10, 12, 13)" .

Cuff

Change to smaller size 4 dp needles. Make sure you have an even number of sts. Work a k1, p1, ribbing for 2" lining up the knit sts and purl sts. Bind off loosely. Slip stitches by lifting them with the right needle from the left needle, one stitch at a time over to the other sleeve section which is between the 3rd and 4th markers attach yarn and follow sleeve directions for second sleeve.

Body

The remaining sts are the body. Attach yarn under arm inseam and join the fronts to the back section at side seams, don't join the front sections. When joining under the arm, pick up 2 sts under each arm to close gap. These extra sts will give ease for cardigan. Continue working Stockinette st working button band and button holes over sts until body measures 6 (8, 9, 10, 10, 11)" or desired length make sure you have an even number of sts. Change to smaller size 4 needles.

Ribbing

With smaller size 4 needles, work k1, p1, decreasing 10 sts evenly around on the first row of ribbing. Cont with ribbing for 2". Bind off loosely.

Finishing

Weave in tail ends and sew on buttons. A blanket st may be worked around buttonholes for reinforcement. Block sweater with water mist and press with hands.

Finished sweater measurements

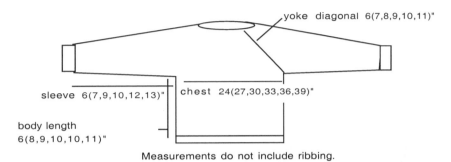

yoke diagonal 6(7,8,9,10,11)"

sleeve 6(7,9,10,12,13)"

chest 24(27,30,33,36,39)"

body length
6(8,9,10,10,11)"

Measurements do not include ribbing.

Ring Around the Cardigan

More Fun Than a Merry Go Round

The checkered ring around the yoke creates a unique contrast for this cardigan. Rolled edges border the cuffs and matching buttons top off this sweater. Knit with worsted weight yarn, this will be a warm and stylish addition for any child's wardrobe.

Sizes

Child's sizes: **2, 4, 6, 8, 10, 12.**
Directions are written for size 2 with larger sizes in parenthesis.

Sweater pictured knit with Paton's Canadiana Tweed & Colours

Finished Chest Measurements

Chest circumference: 24 (27, 30, 33, 36, 39)"

Materials

Yarn Worsted Weight total yardage needed: 420 (500, 600, 750, 800, 950) yds.
Circular Needles One pair each size 4 and 8 16" length. (24" length of each if possible)
Double Point Needles Size 4 and 8.
Markers
Buttons

Gauge

4 to 5 sts and 5 to 6 rows = 1" Stockinette st knit with worsted weight yarn and size 8 needles. Gauge may vary slightly with different yarns.

Note Sweater is knit from the top down on smaller circular needles and as yoke sts increase, longer circular needles are used. Shorter needles will then be used to knit sleeves circular while all other sts remain on longer needles. If sts become too tight, dp needles can be used for remaining sleeve and cuff.

Neck Ribbing

Cast on 80 (84, 88, 92, 96, 100) sts with size 4 needles. Do not join, turn.

Row 1: Knit row, turn.

Row 2: Purl row, turn.

Repeat rows 1 and 2: 3 (3, 4, 4, 5, 5) more times. End WS, wrong side is last row worked. Work 2 rows of k1, p1 ribbing lining up the knit sts and purl sts.

Buttonhole row: Girls buttonhole is on right side, boys on left.

To make buttonhole, cont with ribbing st and at same time work first 3 sts on edge, bind off 2 sts, work to end of row. Turn. Next row, work to where sts were bound off, cast on 2 sts, and continue across row.

Work 2 more rows of k1, p1, ribbing.

Note Throughout the rest of the sweater, work buttonholes every 2" or as often as desired. Make sure you knit first and last 4 (4, 5, 5, 5, 5) sts on every row for entire sweater for button bands.

Preparatory Row (RS) Change to larger size 8 needles and place markers as follows:

K14 (14, 15, 15, 16, 16), place marker, k15 (16, 17, 18, 19, 20), place marker, k22 (23, 24, 25, 26, 27), place marker, k15 (16, 17, 18, 19, 20), place marker, k14 (15, 15, 16, 16, 17), turn. Always slip markers as yoke is knit.

Preparatory Row 2: K4 (4, 5, 5, 5, 5) sts, purl across row to last 4 (4, 5, 5, 5, 5) sts, k last sts, turn.

Optional short row explanation and directions (If you don't want to work short rows, begin with yoke directions) Make sure you are purling on the wrong side of work and knitting on right side. 4 optional short rows may be added to the back and part of the sleeve sections of sweater for a more comfortable fit. Directions are explained here and begin after neck ribbing is finished and you have changed to larger needles and worked preparatory rows. (WS) Slip beg marker (1st marker) and purl to the 4th marker. P2 sts past 4th marker, yarn back (yb), slip 1, yarn forward (yf), turn work to RS, slip 1 st, knit to beg marker, knit 2 sts past beginning marker, yf, sl 1 yb, turn work, WS, sl 1st, purl to where last turn was made (2 sts past the 4th marker) purl 2 more sts, yb, sl 1 st, yf, turn work, RS, sl 1 st, knit to beg marker, knit 2 sts past beg marker, yf, sl 1 yb, turn work, WS, sl 1 st, purl to end of row. Continue with row 1 of yoke.

How to Make1 stitch (M1) On knit side, with left needles, pick up the horizontal strand between last st and next st to be knit. Pick it up from front to back and knit into the back of this strand with the right needle. Strand is twisted to avoid a hole. See notes at beginning of book.

Yoke

Row 1 and all odd rows: (WS) k4 (4, 5, 5, 5, 5) sts, purl across row to last 4 (4, 5, 5, 5, 5) sts, k last sts, turn.

Buttonhole Note Continue to make buttonholes down band as desired, smaller sizes 2" apart works well, 3" for larger sizes. Always work button hole openings 3 sts from edge,

Note The M1 sts will be scattered so the increases don't line up. After the color chart, you can follow the pattern established on rows 2, 4, 6 of pattern or place them where you like. Make sure you work M1 in the same place on each RS row. As more sts are added to the yoke, the M1 can be placed farther away from the markers.

Row 2: Knit row and Make 1 (M1) 2 sts before and after each markers.

Row 4: Knit row and M1 6 sts before and after markers.

Row 6: Knit row and M1 8 sts before and after markers. End WS after row 7.

(RS) Attach contrasting color after button band stitches are worked. Do not work color chart over either button band, only in between. Begin color chart and increases will be worked into chart on row 6. Don't worry about lining up pattern with previous rows

After color chart has been knit through one time, continue knitting yoke in main color working M1's on knit side, alternating their placement. 8 sts will be added each right side (RS) row.

When yoke measures: 6 (7, 8, 9, 10, 11)" end WS.

Knit over to sleeve section which is between the beg marker and the 2nd marker. Leave all other sts on needles, working sleeves over dp or smaller 16" size 8 needles. Smaller sizes will need the dp, larger sizes can use the circular needles.

Sleeve

With dp or size 8 16" circular needles, join sts between beg marker and 2nd marker to knit circular. Place marker where the two sides are joined. Knit circular and every 6th row decrease 1 st before and 1 st after marker by k2tog. Continue knitting sleeve decreasing 1 st before and after marker every 6th row knit sleeve until the underarm inseam measures 6 (8, 10, 11, 12, 14)" or length to wrist without cuff.

Cuff

Change to size 4 dp needles, Make sure you have an even number of sts. Work k1, p1, ribbing lining up k sts and p sts around for 1 1/2" for smaller 3 sizes and 2" for larger 3 sizes. Knit 8 (8, 8, 10, 10, 10) rows of Stockinette st, bind off loosely. Slip sts over to other sleeve section between markers 3 and 4, attach yarn on first stitch. Work second sleeve the same as first.

Body

All remaining sts are body. When joining the fronts and back at the underarm, pick up and knit 2 sts to close gap. On purl side on next row, k2tog twice to reduce those sts added under each arm. Cont with button bands as already established. When body length measures 6 (8, 10, 11, 12, 13)" or desired length, change to smaller size 4 needles and work same directions as for sleeve cuff with ribbing end with knitting rows for rolled edge.

Finishing

Sew on buttons, weave tail ends in and block. You may need to work a reinforcement blanket stitch around the button holes.

Color Chart for Ring Around the Cardigan

Begin with row 1 and work chart once for yoke design, start each row from alternating sides so pattern lines up. Increases will be worked on rows 1 and 6 of chart only, after color chart is complete, cont with increases every other row.

d = dark color.   Lt = light or blank square is light color. Follow the directions within the *'s on those rows indicated.

Row 1	d	d			*K1inc (d), k2 (lt), k2(d), k2(lt),*
Row 2	d	d			Purl side, line up colors
Row 3			d	d	
Row 4			d	d	
Row 5	d	d	d	d	
Row 6	d	d	d	d	* K6, m1,* rep across
Row 7			d	d	
Row 8			d	d	
Row 9	d	d			
Row	d	d			

Finished sweater measurements

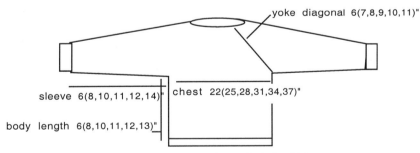

yoke diagonal 6(7,8,9,10,11)"

sleeve 6(8,10,11,12,14)"

chest 22(25,28,31,34,37)"

body length 6(8,10,11,12,13)"

Measurements do not include ribbing.

19

ZigZag
Up's and Down's

Try this variation on the seamless raglan by choosing two contrasting colors, sport weight yarn, and away you go. This sweater can be knit for both boys and girls, change the color and it looks like a different pattern. Knit from the top down, the yoke increases are hidden in the solid colored rows.

Sizes
Child's sizes: **1, 2, 4, 6, 8, 10.**
Instructions are for smallest size with larger sizes in parenthesis.

Sweater pictured knit with Lion Brand Wool Ease

Finished Chest Measurements
Chest circumference: 21 (24, 27, 30, 33, 36)"

Materials
Yarn Sport or dk weight total yardage needed:
Light color MC 300 (400, 500, 600, 800, 850) yds.
Dark color CC 200 (250, 300, 350, 400, 450) yds.
Matching hat one ball of MC and remnants of CC.
Circular Needles One pair each sizes 4 and 6 16" length.
Double Point Needles Size 4 and 6
Markers
Tapestry Needle

Gauge

4 to 5 sts and 6 to 7 rows = 1" knit on size 6 needles in Stockinette st and Wool Ease yarn. Gauge may vary with different yarn.

Neck Ribbing

With size 4 16" circular needles and dark cc yarn, cast on 78 (78, 82, 82, 86, 86) stitches

Row 1: K1, p1; repeat across row. (Do not turn)

Row 2: Place beginning marker on right needle, join beginning of row with end of row to begin circular knitting, make sure stitches are not twisted. Continue with k1, p1, rib pattern slipping marker, until neck ribbing measures 1 1/2" (sizes 1, 2, 4); 2" (sizes 6, 8, 10). End work at beginning marker.

Preparatory Row: Change to larger size 6 16" circular needles, work 1 more row of ribbing placing the markers as follows: Knit and purl 15 (15, 16, 16, 17, 17) sts, place marker, 24 (24, 25, 25, 26, 26) sts, place marker, 15 (15, 16, 16, 17, 17) sts, place marker, 24 (24, 25, 25, 26, 26), beg marker. Sweater is now divided into front, back and sleeves.

Note Start each row from beginning marker and slip markers as you go.

Optional short row explanation and directions (If you don't want to work short rows, begin with yoke directions) 4 optional short rows may be added to the back and part of the sleeve sections of sweater for a more comfortable fit. Directions are explained here and begin after neck ribbing is finished and you have changed to larger needles. Slip beginning marker (1st marker) and knit to the 4th marker. K2 sts past 4th marker, yarn forward (yf), sl 1, yarn back (yb), turn work to wrong side (WS), sl 1 st, purl to beg marker, purl 2 sts past beg marker, yb, sl 1 yf, turn work, right side (RS), sl 1st, knit to where last turn was made (2 sts past the 4th marker) knit 2 more sts, yf, sl 1 st, yb, turn work, WS, sl 1 st, purl to beg marker, purl 2 sts past beg marker, yb, sl 1 yf, turn work, RS, sl 1 st, knit to beg marker.

How to Make 1 stitch (M1) On knit side, with left needles, pick up the horizontal strand between last st and next st to be knit. Pick it up from front to back and knit into the back of this strand with the right needle. Strand is twisted to avoid a hole. See notes at beginning of book.

Yoke

Row 1 and all odd rows: Attach light yarn and begin color chart row 1.

Row 2: Knit row following row 2 of chart and at same time M1 st 2 sts before and after markers. 8 sts will be added on this row. Keep repeating rows 1 to 4 rows of the color chart for the entire yoke, knit row slipping markers as you knit and at same time work the increases as explained next.

Note The M1 sts will be worked in different places each row so the increased sts don't line up. Don't worry about lining up the colors as they line up in the chart. Begin every even multi-colored row with the dark color, either row 1 or 3 of chart.

Row 4: Knit row and at same time M1 4 sts before and after marker. (All odd rows are solid colored.)

Row 6: M1 8 sts before and after marker.

Row 8: M1 2 sts before and after marker.

Row 10: M1 6 st before and after marker.

Row 12: M1 1 sts before and after marker.

Row 14: M1 5 sts before and after marker.

Row 16: M1 9 sts before and after marker.

Row 18: M1 4 sts before and after marker.

M1 sts can be placed farther away from the markers as more sts are added. You can place them where you want as long as they don't line up from row to row. On each increase row make sure they are placed the same number of sts away from the markers . Rep increase rows 1 to 18 for desired length of yoke. Measure along raglan seam not including the neck ribbing. End yoke on either row 1 or 3 of chart, an alternating color row. When yoke measures: 4 (5, 6, 7, 8, 9)" . Work yoke edging pattern from row 1 to 5.

Note The sleeve sections are narrower than front and back and should be the first section worked after beg marker. Sleeves are worked first, keeping all other stitches on needles, just working around sleeve section. Tie off darker contrasting color and keep lighter color for sleeves

Sleeves

Sleeves can be knit circular on smaller size 6 16" needles for larger sizes, or on size 6 dp needles. Slip beg marker and sleeve will be between the beg marker and the 2nd marker.

Row 1: Using dp or 16" size 6 needles, knit sts to next marker, join to knit circular, place marker in center inseam where sleeve sts are joined.

Rows 2 to 5: Knit rows circular.

Row 6: K2tog, knit row to last 2 sts, k2tog.

Continue repeating rows 1 to 6 knitting sleeve circular decreasing 1 stitch before and after marker every 6th row until sleeve inseam is desired arm length, excluding cuff color chart (measure arm inseam) 4 (5, 7, 9, 11)" Tie on contrasting color and work edging chart backwards from row 5 to 1 working from right to left on each row. Next work color chart rows 1 to 3. Make sure you have an even number of sts, and tie off light color.

Cuff

Change to smaller size 4 dp or size 4 16" circular needles, work k1, p1 with dark color and rib stitch lining up knit sts and purl sts for 2". Bind off. Slip stitches on main needle by lifting stitch with the right needle from the left needle over to other sleeve marker which is the 3rd marker. Attach yarn on first stitch and repeat for second sleeve working between the 3rd and 4th markers.

Body

All stitches remaining on needles are the lower sweater body. Attach light yarn on first stitch. Pick up 2 sts in each underarm where front and back are joined to close the small hole between sleeve and body. On next round, k2tog, (knit two sts together) twice under each arm to decrease sts added under arm. Knit circular until body length matches sleeve length or desired length not including pattern or ribbing. Tie on contrasting yarn repeat edging pattern and color chart as was done for sleeves, make sure you have an even number of sts.

Ribbing
Change to smaller size 4 needles, work k1, p1, ribbing for 2". Bind off loosely.

Finishing
Weave tail ends from bottom of sweater and neck edge.

Color Chart Key
D = dark color
Bank square is light color
Work rows 1 to 4 continuously for yoke only, always work from right to left for each row for entire yoke, end on row 1 or 3 of chart when yoke length is completed.

Row 1	D		D	
Row 2	D	D	D	D	Inc row, inc 8
Row 3	D		D	
Row 4				Inc row, inc 8

Edging Pattern for Yoke and Cuffs

D	D	D	D	Row 1
D	D	D	D	Row 2
D	D	D	D	Row 3
D		D	D	Row 4
		D		Row 5

Finished measurements of sweater

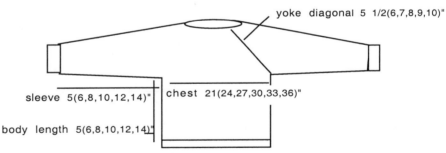

yoke diagonal 5 1/2(6,7,8,9,10)"

sleeve 5(6,8,10,12,14)"   chest 21(24,27,30,33,36)"

body length 5(6,8,10,12,14)"

Measurements do not include ribbing.

Matching ZigZag Hat

Materials
Yarn 200 yds of MC, remnants of CC.
Circular Needles Size 6 16"
Double Point Needles Size 6

Hat
Cast on with MC and size 6 16" circular needles 80 (80, 90, 90, 100, 100) sts, place marker.
Join to knit circular making sure sts are not twisted. Knit circular until piece measures 2 (2, 2, 3, 3, 3)", tie on contrasting yarn. Work 5 rows of color chart starting and ending with a multicolored row either row 1 or 3. Continue with MC for 3 (3, 3, 4, 4, 4)" Begin cap decrease. Change to size 6 dp needles when sts become tight.

Row 1: K8, k2tog; rep around.
Row 2 and every even row: Knit
Row 3: K7, k2tog; rep around.
Row 5: K6, k2tog; rep around.
Row 7: K5, k2tog; rep around.
Row 9: K4, k2tog; rep around.
Row 11: K3, k2tog; rep around.
Row 13: K2, k2tog; rep around.
Row 15: K1, k2tog; rep around.
Row 17: K2tog; rep around.

Cut yarn and with tapestry needle, take yarn back through remaining loops, pull tight, for extra reinforcement, run yarn through sts again. Tie knot on WS and weave end in.

24

Wacky Waves

Colored and Wavy

Sweater is knit in one piece from the neck down. Increases are hidden in the waves, for a smooth yoke. Sizes for this sweater will be determined by the length of the yoke from the neck ribbing to the sleeve inseam. Yarn can vary widely, since gauge isn't a big factor for dimensions.

Sizes
Child's sizes: **1, 2, 4, 6.** Instructions are written for smallest size with larger sizes in parenthesis.

Sweater pictured knit with Mexican Wave Yarn

Finished Chest Measurements
Chest circumference 21 (24, 27, 30)"

Materials
Yarn Sport weight yarn total yardage for main color; black: 400 (500, 600, 700) yds
Remnants of contrasting colors; green, blue, yellow, pink, enough to knit 3 or 4 rows around yoke and cuffs (or colors of your choice).
Circular Needles One pair each circular size 4 and 6 16" length.
Double Point Needles Size 4 and 6.
Tapestry needle
Markers

Hint Use yarn for markers tied in a slip knot. On increase rows, wrap the beginning marker twice to indicate an increase row. Once for non increase row.

Gauge
5 to 6 sts and 7 to 8 rows = 1" Sport weight and size 6 needles knit in Stockinette st. Gauge will vary with texture of yarn.

Neck
With MC cast on 80 (80, 92, 92) sts with size 4 16" circular or dp needles. Turn.
Knit 1,p1, across row, join beginning with end to knit circular, place marker, make sure sts are not twisted.

Ribbing
Row 1 and all rows: K1, p1; rep around to marker. Rep ribbing row lining up knit sts and purl sts until ribbing measures 1 1/2 (1 1/2, 2, 2)" .

Note: For color pattern in yoke, work 5 rows of MC, then 2 rows of contrasting color and repeat for 5 stripes. Color stripes are worked in the following order, but feel free to change it any way you like; blue, green, pink, yellow, green.

Yoke Waves
Note: Work waves pattern until yoke is 5 1/2 (6, 7, 8)" or desired length.
Row 1: Change to larger size 6 needles to knit the yoke. * K3tog, yo, k1, yo,* rep between *'s, continue to beginning marker. There are 20 (20, 24, 24) sections which will be waves. Most rows will end with a yo. Marker may need to be moved a stitch to stay at beg of pattern.
Row 2 and all even rows: Knit row
Row 3: Slip marker, *k1, yo, k3, yo*, (inc row, 40, 40, 48, 48 sts added).
Rows 5, 7, 9, 11: Slip marker, *k1, yo, k1, k3tog, k1, yo,* rep.
Row 13: *K1, yo, k5, yo,* rep. (Inc row)
Rows 15, 17, 19, 21: Slip marker, *k1, yo, k2, k3tog, k2, yo,* rep.
Row 23: *K1, yo, k7, yo,* rep. (Inc row)
Rows 25, 27, 29, 31: Slip marker, *k1, yo, k3, k3tog, k3, yo,* rep.
Row 33: *K1, yo, k9, yo,* rep. (Inc row)
Rows 35, 37, 39, 41: Slip marker, *k1, yo, k4, k3tog, k4, yo,* rep.
Row 43: *K1, yo, k11, yo,* rep. (Inc row)
Rows 45, 47, 49, 51: Slip marker, *k1, yo, k5, k3tog, k5, yo,* rep.
Row 53: *K1, yo, k13, yo,* rep. (Inc row)
Rows 55, 57, 59, 61: Slip marker, *k1, yo, k6, k3tog, k6, yo,* rep.
Row 63: *K1, yo, k15, yo,* rep. (Inc row)

Sleeve
Leave all sts on needle and just work over sleeve sts. These sts will be worked over 4 (4, 5, 5) waves, from the k1, yo, after the marker, over 4 (4, 5, 5) waves to the yo before the k1. When

joining the sleeves, you will have a yo, marker, k1, yo, which will be the inseam. Continue working the last 2 rows of the pattern you worked for the yoke for the next 4 rows making sure non are increase rows.

Sleeve Decrease

Don't work the yo before and after the marker for first sleeve decrease after 4 or 5 rows of sleeve. The next decreases will be worked only into the k3tog sts on either side of the marker. Decreases are worked over a multiple of 6 rows. While continuing the wave pattern, you will work the k3tog every 3rd row on both sides of the marker as established. You will work a k2tog on both sides of the marker every 1st and 5th row. Even rows will be knit.
Work pattern until sleeve is 5 (6, 8, 10)". or desired length without stripes or cuff. Knit 2 rows of contrasting color, 3 rows of MC, 2 rows of another contrasting color, and 3 rows of MC. There should be approx 38 to 48 sts remaining to do cuff, make sure you have an even number of sts.

Ribbing

Change to smaller size 4 needles and work k1, p1, ribbing for 2", bind off loosely. Slip sts from main needles over 6 (6, 7, 7) other waves to yo. Work second sleeve over the next 4 (4, 5, 5) waves, same as other sleeve.

Body

All sts remaining are body, there should be 12 (12, 14, 14) waves remaining. Join front and back and knit circular following same wave pattern until body measures; 6 (7, 9, 11)" Change to smaller size 4 circ needles and work 2" of k1, p1, ribbing. . Bind off loosely.

Finishing

Weave ends in and block flat shaping waves on sleeves and body.

Finished sweater measurements

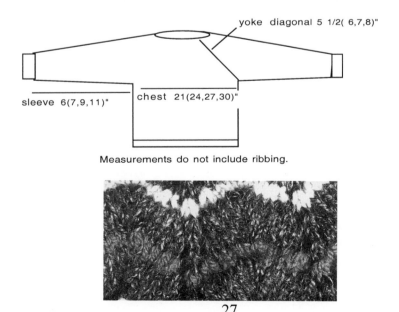

yoke diagonal 5 1/2(6,7,8)"

sleeve 6(7,9,11)"

chest 21(24,27,30)"

Measurements do not include ribbing.

Little
Fair Isle Hood
No Big Bad Wolf

This sweater is knit from the top down, knitting the hood first, then the sweater. The fair isle design dresses up this sweater with a colorful band. With the circular needles, this becomes a fun and quick project.

Sizes
Child's sizes: **1, 2, 4, 6.** Instructions are written for smallest size with larger sizes in parenthesis.

Sweater knit with Plymouth Encore DK yarn.

Finished Chest Measurements
Chest circumference: 22 (25, 28, 31)"

Materials
Yarn DK or sport weight total yardage needed: 400 (450, 550, 750) yds main color
Remnants of dark green, light green, burgundy, gold, brown, blue or 6 colors of your choice.
Circular Needles One pair each size 4 and 6 16"
Double Point Needles Size 4 and 6
Tapestry Needle
Crochet Hook Size D or E

Gauge
5 to 6 sts and 7 to 8 rows = 1" knit with dk weight on size 6 needles and Stockinette st. Gauge will vary with different yarn.

Note When changing colors on hood, knit garter stitch edging first, then tie on next color to avoid knot on outside edge of hood.

Hood

Invisible method of cast on or crocheted chain cast on is best for seaming later but a regular cast on is fine. With size 6 Circular 24" needles, and first color of color chart row 22 cast on 86 (90, 94, 98) sts, turn. Follow color chart from row 22 to row 1 working each row from right to left as you knit the hood, chart is worked backwards from how the yoke is worked.

Row 1: K5, purl to within last 5 sts and knit these last sts, turn.

Row 2: Slip 1st st, knit the rest of row.

Note: Always slip the first st of each row for entire hood and front opening on both rows 1 & 2. Repeat rows 1 and 2 for 8 (9, 10, 11)". You may want to measure top of head to neck for this measurement. On last row (RS), decrease 10 sts evenly across by k2tog. Total sts 76 (80, 84, 88). Change to smaller size 4 needles.

Neck Ribbing

Row 1 (WS): K5 *p1, k1*, There will be a ribbing where the p stitches and k sts line up. rep between *'s to last 5 sts, knit these sts, turn.

Row 2 (RS): K5, *k1, p1*, Line up the k sts and p sts. Rep between *'s to last 5 sts, knit these sts, turn. Rep ribbing rows 1 and 2 for 1 1/2 (1 1/2, 2, 2)" end WS turn.

Yoke

Preparatory row: (RS) Change to larger size 6 needles. K13 (14, 15, 15), place marker, k14 (14, 15, 16), place marker, k22 (24, 24, 25), place marker, k14 (14, 15, 16), place marker, k13 (14, 15, 16). Total sts: 76 (80, 84, 88)

Rows 1, 3, 5, 7, 9: (WS) K5, p to within last 5 sts, k these sts.

Row 2: (RS) and all even rows: Knit row working M1 2 sts before and after each marker.

Row 4: Repeat row 2 except M1 6 sts before and after markers.

Row 6: Repeat row 2 except M1 3 sts before and after markers.

Row 8, 10, 12, 14: Repeat row 2 and M1 in alternating places so they don't line up. As more sts are added, the M1 can be placed farther away from marker. End WS.

Join Placket Note: You will continue to increase yoke every other row after placket is joined and throughout the color chart. (RS) Join the front sections to knit circular overlapping front garter sts. Place the last 5 sts on a dp needle. Hold behind the first 5 sts and knit both sets of 5 sts together at same time by placing needle through both loops at the same time and treating as one stitch. Begin color chart after placket is joined for fair isle pattern. Continue to knit front circular until yoke measures 6 (7, 8, 9)" not including neck ribbing.

Sleeve

With size 6 dp needles, work over sleeve sts which will be between the first and second marker. Join to knit circular and place marker where sts are joined at sleeve inseam.

Rows 1 to 5: Knit

Row 6: K2tog after marker, knit row and k2tog in 2 sts before marker.

Repeat rows 1 to 6 until sleeve inseam measures: 6 (7, 9, 11)" making sure you end with an even number of sts.

Cuff

Change to smaller size 4 dp needles to do ribbing. Work a k1, p1, ribbing for 2" lining up the knit and purl sts. Bind off loosely. Slip sts from the main needles over to the other sleeve section, slip each stitch from the left needle to the right needle, until you are at the other sleeve section between the 3rd and 4th markers. Attach yarn and repeat sleeve directions for second sleeve.

Body

All sts remaining are body. Join front and back to knit circular. When joining front to back, pick up 2 to 3 sts under arm to close gap under arm. Continue knitting body until it measures 5 (6, 7, 8)" or desired length. Change to smaller size 4 circular or dp needles. Work k1, p1, ribbing for 2 (2, 3, 3)" lining up the knit and purl sts. Bind off loosely

Finishing

Weave ends in. With one of the contrasting colors and crochet hook work a single crochet edge around the opening of the placket and hood. For a more textured edge, work the single crochet edge backwards, instead of working to the left, work each stitch to the right. This will create a twist and a nubby edge.

Finished sweater measurements

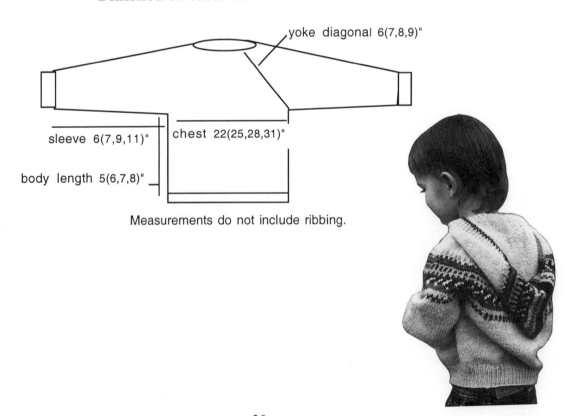

yoke diagonal 6(7,8,9)"

sleeve 6(7,9,11)"

chest 22(25,28,31)"

body length 5(6,7,8)"

Measurements do not include ribbing.

Color Key

	Light mc
g	Lt.green
R	Dk.red
b	blue
D	Dk.green
B	Brown
y	yellow

Color Chart

Start each row from the right side and work to left, repeat around row.

Work chart rows 1 through 22.

g		g		Row 1
g		g		2
	r		r	3
r	b	r	b	4
b	b	b	b	5
G	G	G	G	6
g	g	g	g	7
g	B	g	B	8
y	B	y	B	9
y	g	y	g	10
y	r	y	r	11
r	r	r	r	12
	G	G	G	13
G		G	G	14
G	G		G	15
b		b	b	16
b	b	b	b	17
b	b	b	b	18
				19
y		y		20
B	y	B	y	21
B	y	B	y	22

Bright Heart Set

Says "I Love You"

Knit with dark yarn and contrasting bright motifs, this sweater set will brighten any child's day. The yoke increases are worked between the motifs for a seamless raglan effect. Bright and cheery for any little girl

Sizes
Child's sizes: **1**, **2**, **4**, **6**. Instructions are written for smallest size with larger sizes in parenthesis.

Sweater pictured knit with Mexican Wave Yarn

Finished Chest Measurements
Chest circumference: 22 (25, 28, 31)"

Materials
Yarn Sport weight yarn total yardage needed for Main color black: 400 (450, 550, 650) yds. Remnants of green, blue, yellow and pink for Contrasting colors.
Circular Needles One pair each size 4 and 6 16"
Double Point Needles Size 4 and 6.
Markers

Gauge
5 to 6 sts and 7 to 8 rows = 1" knit with sport weight and size 6 needles in Stockinette st. Gauge will vary with texture of yarn.

Neck ribbing

Cast on 80 (84, 88, 92) sts with size 4 16" circular or dp needles. Turn.

Knit across row, join beginning with end to knit circular, place marker, make sure sts are not twisted. Knit 6 rows of Stockinette st, end at marker.

Ribbing Row: K2, p2; rep around to marker. Rep ribbing row 5 more times. 6 rows total. Change to larger size 6 needles and knit preparatory row.

Preparatory Row: Slip beginning marker, K16 (17, 18, 19), place marker, k24 (25, 26, 27), place marker, k16 (17, 18, 19), place marker, k24 (25, 26, 27).

Optional short row explanation and directions (If you don't want to work short rows, begin with yoke directions) 4 optional short rows may be added to the back and part of the sleeve sections of sweater for a more comfortable fit. Directions are explained here and begin after neck ribbing is finished and you have changed to larger needles. Slip beginning marker (1st marker) and knit to the 4th marker. K2 sts past 4th marker, yarn forward (yf), sl 1, yarn back (yb), turn work to WS, sl 1 st, purl to beg marker, purl 2 sts past beginning marker, yb, sl 1 yf, turn work, RS, sl 1st, knit to where last turn was made (2 sts past the 4th marker) knit 2 more sts, yf, sl 1 st, yb, turn work, WS, sl 1 st, purl to beg marker, purl 2 sts past beg marker, yb, sl 1 yf, turn work, RS, sl 1 st, knit to beg marker.

How to Make1 stitch (M1) On knit side, with left needles, pick up the horizontal strand between last st and next st to be knit. Pick it up from front to back and knit into the back of this strand with the right needle. Strand is twisted to avoid a hole. See pattern notes for illustration.

Begin Color Chart and follow increase instructions at same time. Don't worry if you have an extra color stitch where you worked the M1, overall, it won't really show. M1's may need to be shifted a little to be done in between the heart and flower motifs.

Row 1 and all odd rows: Knit.

Row 2: M1, 2 sts before and after each marker.

Row 4: M1 8 sts before and after markers.

Row 6: M1 4 sts before and after markers.

Row 8: M1 1 sts before and after markers.

You can rep rows 1 to 8 for increases or work the M1 farther away from the markers as more sts are added. Be consistent in their placement on each row and work the the same distance from each marker on that particular row. Make sure they are staggered from row to row so they don't line up. When yoke (not including ribbing) measures 5 1/2 (6, 7, 8)" knit to beginning marker to start sleeve.

Sleeve

Note All sts will remain on needle while sleeve sts are worked on separate needles. DP needles can be used to knit sleeves circular, or they can be knit on RS and purled on WS and seamed up when finished.

Rows 1 to 5: Knit

Row 6: k2tog before and after marker knitting the rest of the row. Continue working rows 1 to 6 until sleeve inseam measures 6 (7, 9, 11)".

Change to smaller size 4 dp needles and work k2, p2, ribbing for 6 rows. K6 rows of Stockinette st. bind off loosely. Slip sts over to other sleeve sts between markers 3 and 4. Work second sleeve the same.

Body
All sts remaining are body, when joining the front and back pick up 2 sts under each arm inseam to help close the gap. On the next round, k2tog 2 times to decrease these extra sts. Knit body circular until body meas. 6 (7, 9, 11)".

Ribbing
Change to smaller size 4 dp needles and work 6 rows of k2, p2, ribbing. A few sts may need to be decreased to have a multiple of 4 sts for ribbing to work. K5 rows of Stockinette st. Bind off.

Finishing
Weave ends in and block flat.

Finished sweater measurements

Color Key

y	yellow
b	blue
p	pink
g	green
B	Black

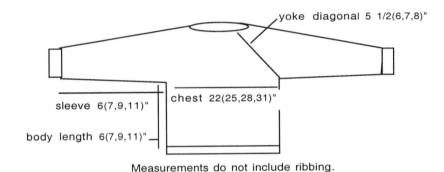

yoke diagonal 5 1/2(6,7,8)"

sleeve 6(7,9,11)"

chest 22(25,28,31)"

body length 6(7,9,11)"

Measurements do not include ribbing.

Color Chart
Work each row from right to left.

g	B	g	B	1
B	B	B	B	2
B	B	B	B	3
B	B	y	B	4
B	y	b	y	5
y	b	b	b	6
b	b	b	b	7
b	b	b	b	8

b	p	p	b	p	p	b	b	9
p	p	p	p	p	p	p	b	10
p	p	p	p	p	p	p	b	11
b	p	p	p	p	p	b	b	12
b	b	b	p	p	b	b	b	13
b	b	b	p	b	b	b	b	14

g	g	g	g	15
B	g	B	g	16
g	B	g	B	17
B	B	B	B	18
B	B	B	B	19
y	y	y	y	20
y	y	y	p	21
p	y	p	b	22
y	y	y	p	23
y	y	y	g	24
g	B	g	B	25
B	b	B	b	26
b	b	b	b	27
y	y	y	y	28
p	p	p	p	29
B	B	B	B	30
y	p	p	p	31
B	B	g	B	32
B	B	B	B	33

Bright Heart Hat

Yarn 1 100 gr ball of MC, remnants of CC.
Circular Needles Size 6 16" length
Double Point Needles Size 6

Cast on with MC and size 6 circular needles; 80 (80, 90, 90, 100, 100) sts, place marker.
Join to knit circular making sure sts are not twisted. Knit circular until work measures 2 (2, 2, 3, 3, 3)", tie on contrasting yarn.

Follow rows 15 to 33 of color chart working each row from right to left. Continue with MC for 2 (2, 2, 3, 3, 3)" Begin cap decrease. Change to size 6 dp needles when sts become tight.
Row 1: K8, k2tog; rep around.
Row 2 and every even row: Knit
Row 3: K7, k2tog; rep around.
Row 5: K6, k2tog; rep around.
Row 7: K5, k2tog; rep around.
Row 9: K4, k2tog; rep around.

Row 11: K3, k2tog; rep around.
Row 13: K2, k2tog; rep around.
Row 15: K1, k2tog; rep around.
Row 17: K2tog; rep around.
With tapestry needle, take yarn back through remaining loops, pull tight and secure.

Crayon Pullover
Color it Carefully

This colorful sweater will add cheer to any outfit as well as make a warm addition on a cool day. Sport weight yarn, knit with a variety of red, yellow, blue, white and green, creates a bright yoke for any child. Only 2 colors are knit at one time and the increases are built in to the color chart .

Sizes
Child's sizes: **2, 4, 6, 8, 10, 12.** Instructions are written for smallest size with larger sizes in parenthesis.

Sweater pictured knit with Plymouth Encore dk yarn

Finished Chest Measurements
Chest circumference: 22 (25, 28, 31, 34, 37)"

Materials
Yarn dk weight total yardage needed: 400 (500, 600, 700, 800, 1000) yds.
Yoke colors: red, yellow, white, green; one 50 gr ball of each
Circular Needles One pair each size 4 and 6 16" length , size 6 24" length.
Double Point Needles Size 4 and 6
Markers

Gauge
5 to 6 sts and 7 to 8 rows =1" knit with dk yarn and Stockinette st on size 6 needles. Gauge will vary with different yarns.

Top Neck Edge

With smaller size 4 circular needles cast on 76 (76, 80, 80, 84, 84) sts.

Join to knit circular make sure stitches are not twisted.

Row 1: K2, p2, repeat around, place beg marker when joining.

Row 2: K2, p2, making sure knit sts line up an purl sts line up. Continue with this ribbing pattern until ribbing measures 2 (2, 2, 2, 3, 3)". On last row evenly increase the following number of stitches by working a k1inc in the second knit stitch of the k2; 5 (5, 4, 4, 3, 3) stitches. Change to larger size 6 needles and place a marker at the beginning of the row.

Optional short row explanation and directions (If you don't want to work short rows, begin with yoke directions) 4 optional short rows may be added to the back and part of the sleeve sections of sweater for a more comfortable fit. Directions are explained here and begin after neck ribbing is finished and you have changed to larger needles. Slip beginning marker (1st marker) and knit to the 4th marker. K2 sts past 4th marker, yarn forward (yf), sl 1, yarn back (yb), turn work to WS, sl 1 st, purl to beg marker, purl 2 sts past beginning marker, yb, sl 1 yf, turn work, RS, sl 1st, knit to where last turn was made (2 sts past the 4th marker) knit 2 more sts, yf, sl 1 st, yb, turn work, WS, sl 1 st, purl to beg marker, purl 2 sts past beg marker, yb, sl 1 yf, turn work, RS, sl 1 st, knit to beg marker.

How to Make1 stitch (M1) On knit side, with left needles, pick up the horizontal strand between last st and next st to be knit. Pick it up from front to back and knit into the back of this strand with the right needle. Strand is twisted to avoid a hole. See pattern notes for detailed pictures.

Yoke

Each repeat of the chart will be a section. As the yoke sts increase, the sections become wider. There are 27 (27, 28, 28, 29, 29) sections that are repeated. At the beginning of the chart there will be 81 (81, 84, 84, 87, 87) sts. Begin following color chart starting each round from the right side, or the straight edge of the chart. On every 6th row of the chart, increase one st when chart indicates by k1inc in last color st where chart has an extra st. Continue this increase this for every repeat of the section. 27 (27, 28, 28, 29, 29) sts will be added on this round and each increase round. When Yoke measures 6 (7, 8, 9, 10, 11)", there should be approx. 270 (297, 336, 364, 406, 435) sts. Sweater will be divided for sleeve, front,sleeve, and back as follows:

Front and back sections have approx 20 sts more than the sleeves.

Size 2: 57, 78, 57, 78. (270 stitches total)

Size 4: 64, 84, 64, 85. (297 stitches total)

Size 6: 74, 94, 74, 94 (336 stitches total)

Size 8: 81, 101, 81, 101 (364 stitches total)

Size 10: 92, 111, 92, 111 (406 stitches total)

Size 12: 99, 118, 99, 119 (435 stitches total)

Sleeves

From beg marker, MC and 16" size 6 circular or dp needles, k57 (64, 74, 81, 92, 99) sts, join to knit circular. Place marker when joining.

Rows 1 to 5: Knit 5 rows circular

Row 6: Knit row and at same time decrease 1 st before and after marker by k2tog. Continue to decrease one st on each side of marker every 6th row by k2tog. Knit sleeve until it measures 6 (8, 10, 12, 13, 14)" follow cuff chart. Change to smaller size 4 dp needles, work k1, p1, ribbing for 2 (2, 2, 3, 3)" Bind off loosely. Skip over 78 (84, 94, 101, 111, 118) sts, and repeat for other sleeve working over 57 (64, 74, 81, 92, 99) sts.

Body

All remaining sts are body. Front and back sections will be joined to knit circular. When connecting under arm, pick up 2 sts to close gap, then k2tog twice on the next round. Join yarn and knit body circular to match length of sleeve or desired length without the cuff.

Cuff

Change to smaller size 4 circular needles, decrease 10 sts evenly across first row of k1, p1 ribbing. Work ribbing to match sleeves 2 (2, 2, 3, 3)" bind off loosely.

Finishing

Weave in loose ends and block.

Sleeve Cuff Color Chart

w	w	b	1
w	w	y	2
w	w	y	3
r	r	g	4
w	w	t	5
w	w	b	6

Finished sweater measurements

yoke diagonal 6(7,8,9,10,11)"

sleeve 6(7,9,10,12,13)"

chest 22(25,28,31,34,37)"

body length 6(8,9,10,10,11)"

Measurements do not include ribbing.

Yoke Color Key

Begin on right top corner and always work from right to left on each row. Start from the straight edge and work towards the side that widens. On the row with an extra step, about every 6th row, work a K1 inc with the last color for that row or color indicated by chart.

w	White
y	Yellow
r	Red
g	Green
b	Blue

Color Chart for Crayon Pullover

Start each row from right side and repeat around row.
End Color Chart when yoke is desired
length for size.

																				b	w	w	**1**
																				b	w	w	**2**
																				b	w	w	**3**
																				b	w	w	**4**
																				b	y	y	**5**
																			b	b	y	y	**6**
																			b	b	w	w	**7**
																			b	b	w	w	**8**
																			b	b	w	w	**9**
																			b	b	w	w	**10**
																			b	b	w	w	**11**
																			r	r	r	w	w	**12**
																			r	r	r	w	w	**13**
																			b	b	b	b	w	**14**
																			g	g	b	g	g	**15**
																			g	g	b	g	g	**16**
																			w	w	y	w	w	**17**
																		y	w	w	y	w	w	**18**
																		b	r	r	b	r	r	**19**
																		y	w	w	y	w	w	**20**
																		y	w	w	y	w	w	**21**
																		b	g	g	b	g	g	**22**
																		r	w	w	r	w	w	**23**
																	r	r	w	w	r	w	w	**24**
																b	b	y	y	b	y	y	**25**
																b	b	y	y	b	y	y	**26**
																b	b	w	w	b	w	w	**27**

						b	b	w	w	b	w	w	28
						b	b	w	w	b	w	w	29
					g	g	g	w	w	g	w	w	30
					g	g	g	w	w	g	w	w	31
					r	r	r	w	w	r	w	w	32
					r	r	r	g	g	r	g	g	33
					b	b	b	g	g	b	g	g	34
					y	y	y	w	w	y	w	w	35
				y	y	y	y	w	w	y	w	w	36
				r	b	b	b	r	r	b	r	r	37
				w	y	y	y	w	w	y	w	w	38
				w	y	y	y	w	w	y	w	w	39
				g	b	b	b	g	g	b	g	g	40
			w	w	r	r	r	w	w	r	w	w	41
			r	w	r	r	r	w	w	r	w	w	42 Size 2
			b	y	b	b	b	y	y	b	y	y	43
			b	y	b	b	b	y	y	b	y	y	44
			b	w	b	b	b	w	w	b	w	w	45
			b	w	b	b	b	w	w	b	w	w	46
			b	w	b	b	b	w	w	b	w	w	47
		r	r	w	r	r	r	w	w	r	w	w	48
		r	r	w	r	r	r	w	w	r	w	w	49 size 4
		g	g	w	g	g	g	w	w	g	w	w	50
		g	g	b	g	g	g	b	b	g	b	b	51
		g	g	b	g	g	g	b	b	g	b	b	52
		y	y	w	y	y	y	w	w	y	w	w	53
		y	y	w	y	y	y	w	w	y	w	w	54
	b	b	b	r	b	b	b	r	r	b	r	r	55
	w	y	y	w	y	y	y	w	w	y	w	w	56 size 6
	w	y	y	w	y	y	y	w	w	y	w	w	57
	w	b	b	w	b	b	b	w	w	b	w	w	58
	w	r	r	w	r	r	r	w	w	r	w	w	59
	w	r	r	w	r	r	r	w	w	r	w	w	60
	y	b	b	y	b	b	b	y	y	b	y	y	61
	y	b	b	y	b	b	b	y	y	b	y	y	62
b	w	b	b	w	b	b	b	w	w	b	w	w	63 size 8
b	w	b	b	w	b	b	b	w	w	b	w	w	64
b	w	b	b	w	b	b	b	w	w	b	w	w	65
b	w	b	b	w	b	b	b	w	w	b	w	w	66
r	w	r	r	w	r	r	r	w	w	r	w	w	67
r	w	r	r	w	r	r	r	w	w	r	w	w	68

				g	g	b	g	g	b	g	g	g	b	b	g	b	b	**69**
				g	g	b	g	g	b	g	g	g	b	b	g	b	b	**70 size 10**
				y	y	w	y	y	w	y	y	y	w	w	y	w	w	**71**
				y	y	w	y	y	w	y	y	y	w	w	y	w	w	**72**
				b	b	w	b	b	w	b	b	b	w	w	b	w	w	**73**
				b	b	w	b	b	w	b	b	b	w	w	b	w	w	**74**
			r	r	r	w	r	r	w	r	r	r	w	w	r	w	w	**75**
			r	r	r	w	r	r	w	r	r	r	w	w	r	w	w	**76**
			g	g	g	y	g	g	y	g	g	g	y	y	g	y	y	**77 size 12**

Circumnavigate
Sailing the Fair Isle

Knit this Green Tweed sweater with worsted weight Canadiana yarn for extra warmth. Knit from the neck down in one piece, any boy or girl will enjoy this pullover for dress or play. The yoke increases are made by working Make 1 sts and with the tweed yarn, or any yarn with texture or various colors, the increases are hidden in the yoke for a smooth look. The contrasting stripe is also worked with worsted weight yarn, any colors can be substituted for individuality.

Sizes
Child's sizes: **2, 4, 6, 8, 10, 12.** Instructions are written for smallest size with larger sizes in parenthesis.

Sweater pictured knit with Patons Canadiana yarn

Finished Chest Measurements
Chest circumference: 22 (25, 28, 31, 34, 37)"

Materials
Yarn Patons Worsted weight total yardage needed of Main color; 420 (500, 600, 700, 800, 900) yds.
50 grams of the following colors: gold, off white , burgundy, blue, light green,
Circular Needles One pair each size 4 and 8 16", Size 8 24" circular needles
Double Point Needles Size 4 and 8.
Markers

Gauge
4 to 5 sts and 6 to 7 rows = 1" knit with worsted weight yarn on size 8 needles in Stockinette st. Gauge will vary with different yarns.

Top Neck Edge
With size 4 circular needles, cast on 76 (80, 80, 84, 84, 88).
Row 1: K2, P2, repeat across row. (do not turn)
Row 2: Place beginning marker on right needle, join beg of row with end of row to begin circular knitting, make sure sts are not twisted. Continue with k2, p2, rib pattern, slip beg marker. Work until neck ribbing measures 1" (sizes 2, 4, 6) 2" (sizes 8, 10, 12). End work at beginning marker.

Yoke
Change to larger size 8 needles and knit one row and place markers as follows:
K15 (16, 16, 17, 17, 18), place marker, k23 (24, 24, 25, 25, 26), place marker, k15 (16, 16, 17, 17, 18), place marker, k23 (24, 24, 25, 25, 26) place marker.

Optional short row explanation and directions (If you don't want to work short rows, begin with yoke directions) 4 optional short rows may be added to the back and part of the sleeve sections of sweater for a more comfortable fit. Directions are explained here and begin after neck ribbing is finished and you have changed to larger needles. Slip beg marker (1st marker) and knit to the 4th marker. K2 sts past 4th marker, yf, sl 1, yb, turn work to WS, sl 1 st, purl to beg marker, purl 2 sts past beg marker, yb, sl 1 yf, turn work, RS, sl 1st, knit to where last turn was made (2 sts past the 4th marker) knit 2 more sts, yf, sl 1 st, yb, turn work, WS, sl 1 st, purl to beg marker, purl 2 sts past beg marker, yb, sl 1 yf, turn work, RS, sl 1 st, knit to beg marker.

How to Make1 stitch (M1) On knit side, with left needles, pick up the horizontal strand between last st and next st to be knit. Pick it up from front to back and knit into the back of this strand with the right needle. Strand is twisted to avoid a hole. See pattern notes for detailed pictures.

Yoke Increase
Increases are scattered so they do not line up. They are placed in different places each increase row, but still worked the same number of sts from marker for that row. Stitches are increased by working Make 1.
Row 1: Slip beg marker, k4, M1, Continue knitting circular with a M1, 4 sts before and after each marker. End at beg marker. 8 sts added.
Row 2 and all even rows: Knit.
Row 3: Knit row and work a M1, 1 sts before and after markers (bam).
Row 5: Knit row and work a M1, 4 sts bam.
Row 7: Knit row and work a M1, 6 sts bam.
Row 9: Knit row and work a M1, 1 st bam.
Row 11: knit row and work a M1, 10 sts bam
Continue in this pattern repeating rows 1 to 11. You can place the M1 where you want and as

more sts are added, they can be placed farther from the markers, until yoke measures ribbing not included 4 (5, 6, 7, 8, 9)". Begin color chart and continue with increases on odd rows. Until yoke measures 6 (7, 8, 9, 10, 11)" not including ribbing.

Sleeves

Slip beginning marker, with size 4 dp needles for smaller sized sweaters, or smaller size 4 16" circular needles, sleeve sts are between the beg marker and the 2nd marker. Join beg with end, place marker. Continue color chart and work decrease while sleeve is knit. After color chart, cont knitting sleeve in main color working decreases.

Decreases: Knit 5 rows. On 6th row, knit 2 sts together, knit to within 2 sts of marker and k2tog. Slip marker. Repeat this pattern of decreasing 2 sts every 6th row until arm inseam measures; 6 (7, 9, 11, 13, 14)" making sure you have a multiple of 4 sts.

Cuff

Change to smaller size 4 circular or dp needles, work in k2, p2 ribbing stitch for 1 (1, 1, 2, 2, 2)" Bind off loosely. Slip stitches on needle over to other sleeve sts between the 3rd and 4th markers. Attach yarn on first stitch and repeat sleeve directions.

Body

Remaining sts are body. Front and back will be joined to knit circular. Begin color Chart and on first row under each arm pick up 2 sts to close gap. On next round, k2tog 2 times under each arm to decrease the added sts. After color chart continue to knit in MC.
Knit body the same length as sleeves or desired length. Change to smaller size 4 needles. Work k2, p2, ribbing for 2 (2, 2, 3, 3, 3)" bind off loosely.

Finishing

Weave in tail ends and block.

Finished measurements for sweater

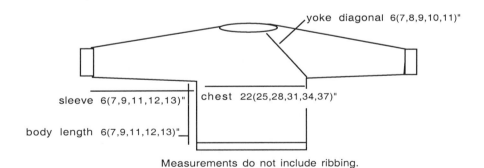

Measurements do not include ribbing.

45

Color Key

	Off White
g	Lt Green
y	Yellow
r	Dk Red
G	Dk. Green
b	Blue

Color Chart for Circumnavigate

Begin each row of color chart from
right and work left.

g	G	G	1
G	g	G	2
G	G	g	3
G	r	G	4
r	r	r	5
r	r	r	6
r	y		7
y	r		8
y	y		9
y	y		10
y	y	b	11
y	b	y	12
b	y	y	13
G	G	G	14
g	g	g	15
r	r	r	16
b	b	b	17
y	g		18
g	y		19
g	r		20
g	G		21
G	g		

YUM YUM GREENS

Can't Grow This in Your garden

Sweater pictured knit wih Plymouth Encore dk

Try this variation on the seamless raglan. Combining shades of green and yellow with a base of tan, the colors blend for a sophisticated expression. Increases are worked in the color fair isle pattern for a smooth flowing yoke.

Sizes

Child's sizes: **2, 4, 6, 8, 10.** Instructions are written for the smallest size with larger sizes in parenthesis.

Finished Chest Measurements

Chest circumference: 22 (25, 28, 31, 34, 37)"

Materials

Yarn DK or sport weight total yardage needed of Main Color: 450 (550, 650, 750, 850) yds.
1 ball of each color dk green, green, yellow or 3 contrasting colors of your choice.
Circular Needles One pair each size 4 and 6 16" size 6 24" circular needles.
Double Point Needles Size 4 and 6.
Markers
Tapestry Needle

Gauge

5 to 6 sts and 7 to 8 rows = 1" knit with dk weight yarn in Stockinette st with size 6 needles. Gauge will vary with different yarns.

Neck Ribbing

With size 4 16" circular needles, cast on 78 (78, 82, 82, 86, 86) stitches, turn.

Row 1: K1, P1, repeat across row. (do not turn)

Row 2: Place beginning marker (on right needle, join beginning of row with end of row to begin circular knitting, make sure stitches are not twisted. Continue with K1, p1, rib pattern lining up knit and purl sts, slipping marker until neck ribbing measures 2 (2, 2, 3, 3, 3)". End work at beginning marker. Work 1 more row of ribbing placing the markers as follows: Knit and purl 15 (15, 16, 16, 17, 17) sts, place marker, 24 (24, 25, 25, 26, 26) sts, place marker, 15 (15, 16, 16, 17, 17) sts, place marker, 24 (24, 25, 25, 26, 26), beginning marker.

Yoke

Change to larger size 6 16" circular needles. Sweater is now divided into front, back and sleeves.

Note Start each row from beg marker and slip markers as you go.

Row 1: Knit row and at same time M1 st, 2 sts before and after each marker. 8 sts will be added on this row.

Optional short row explanation and directions (If you don't want to work short rows, begin with yoke directions) 4 optional short rows may be added to the back and part of the sleeve sections of sweater for a more comfortable fit. Directions are explained here and begin after neck ribbing is finished and you have changed to larger needles. Slip beginning marker (1st marker) and knit to the 4th marker. K2 sts past 4th marker, yarn forward (yf), sl 1, yarn back (yb), turn work to WS, sl 1 st, purl to beg marker, purl 2 sts past beginning marker, yb, sl 1 yf, turn work, RS, sl 1st, knit to where last turn was made (2 sts past the 4th marker) knit 2 more sts, yf, sl 1 st, yb, turn work, WS, sl 1 st, purl to beg marker, purl 2 sts past beg marker, yb, sl 1 yf, turn work, RS, sl 1 st, knit to beg marker.

How to Make1 stitch (M1) On knit side, with left needles, pick up the horizontal strand between last st and next st to be knit. Pick it up from front to back and knit into the back of this strand with the right needle. Strand is twisted to avoid a hole. See pattern notes for illustrations.

Row 1: Start color chart, knit row and M1 2 sts before and after markers.

Row 2 and all even rows : Knit row slipping markers as you knit.

Note The M1 sts will be worked in different places each row so the increased sts don't line up. Make sure you add them in the same place on each row. Follow the color chart, there will be places where increases are made that will temporarily offset the pattern, try to line it up as best as possible but it won't really show when yoke is complete.

Row 3: M1 4 sts before and after markers.

Row 5: M1 8 sts before and after markers.

Row 7: M1 2 sts before and after markers.

Row 9: M1 6 st before and after markers.

Rep inc rows 1 to 9 for desired length of yoke. M1 sts can be placed farther away from the markers as more sts are added. Measure along front raglan section not including the neck ribbing for the following sizes: 6 (7, 8, 9, 10, 11)".

Note The sleeve sections are narrower than front and back and should be the first section worked after beginning marker. Sleeves are worked first, keeping all other stitches on needles, just working around sleeve section.

Sleeves

Slip beginning marker, Sleeves can be knit circular on smaller size 6 16" needles,or on size 6 dp needles.

Row 1: Using dp or 16" size 6 needles circular needles, k sts from beg marker to 2nd marker, join to knit circular, place marker in center inseam where sleeve sts were joined.

Rows 1 to 5: Knit rows circular.

Row 6: While knitting row, k2tog before and after marker.

Continue knitting sleeve circular dec 1 st before and after marker every 6th row.

Repeat decrease pattern until sleeve inseam is 6 (8, 10, 12, 13, 14)" or desired arm length, excluding cuff color chart measure arm Tie on contrasting color and work color chart for cuff. Make sure you have an even number of sts.

Cuff

Change to smaller size 4 dp, work in K1, p1 rib stitch 2" lining up the knit and purl sts. Bind off. Slip stitches on needle over to other sleeve sts between the 3rd and 4th markers. Attach yarn on first stitch and repeat for second sleeve.

Body

All stitches remaining on needles are the lower sweater body. Attach yarn on first stitch. Pick up 2 sts in each underarm where front and back are joined to close the small hole between sleeve and body. On next round, k2tog, twice under each arm to decrease sts added under arm. Knit circular until body length matches sleeve length or desired length, not including pattern or ribbing. Tie on contrasting yarn work cuff color chart. Make sure you have an even number of remaining sts.

Ribbing

Change to smaller size 4 needles, work k1, p1, ribbing for 2" lining up the knit and purl sts. Bind off loosely.

Finishing

Weave tail ends from bottom of sweater and neck edge. Block with water mist and press with hands.

Matching Hat

Materials

Yarn 180 yds of Main Color
 Remnants of other colors.
Needles Size 6 16" and size 6 dp needles.

Ribbing

Cast on with MC 80 (80, 90, 90, 100, 100)sts. Place marker.

Join to knit circular making sure sts are not twisted. Place marker where joined.

Row 1: K1, p1; rep around to beginning marker. Repeat row 1 until ribbing measures 1 1/2" to 2". Begin cuff color chart from sweater pattern working chart from the right side to left one time. Knit circular with MC until hat measures; 6 (6, 6 1/2, 6 1/2, 7, 7)" not including ribbing.

Row 1: K8, k2tog; rep around.

Row 2 and every even row: Knit

Row 3: K7, k2tog; rep around.

Row 5: K6, k2tog; rep around.

Row 7: K5, k2tog; rep around.

Row 9: K4, k2tog; rep around.

Row 11: K3, k2tog; rep around.

Row 13: K2, k2tog; rep around.

Row 15: K1, k2tog; rep around.

Row 17: K2tog; rep around.

Note Several finishing touches can be worked here. Listed below are the options.

A. Cut yarn and with tapestry needle, take yarn back through remaining loops, pull tight, for extra reinforcement, run yarn through sts again. Tie knot on WS and cut.

B. Take remaining 5 to 6 sts and with same size dp or circular needle as ribbing was worked, work an I cord for 3", tie the I cord in a loose knot.

C. Follow directions on A, then make a pompom with the various colors and attach to top of hat.

Finished sweater measurements

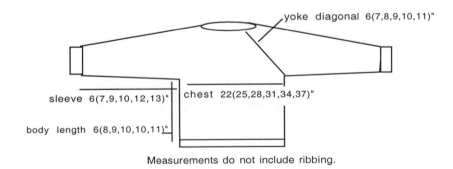

yoke diagonal 6(7,8,9,10,11)"

sleeve 6(7,9,10,12,13)"

chest 22(25,28,31,34,37)"

body length 6(8,9,10,10,11)"

Measurements do not include ribbing.

Color Key

y	Yellow
	Tan
g	Lt. Green
G	Dk. Green

Color Chart

Row 1 begin top left corner and continue to
begin each row from the left side and repeat around.
Start each row from right side and work to the left, the same direction you are knitting.

t	t	t	t	1	t	t	t	t	17	g	t	g	t	33
y	t	y	t	2	t	t	t	t	18	G	t	G	t	34
y	y	y	y	3	t	t	y	y	19	G	G	G	G	35
y	y	y	y	4	t	t	y	y	20	G	G	G	G	36
g	y	g	y	5	y	y	g	g	21	G	G	t	t	37
g	g	g	g	6	y	y	g	g	22	G	G	t	t	38 end size 2
g	g	g	g	7	g	g	g	g	23	y	y	y	y	39
g	g	G	G	8	G	g	G	g	24	y	y	y	y	40
g	g	G	G	9	g	G	g	G	25	y	t	y	t	41
G	G			10	G	y	G	y	26	t	G	t	G	42
G	G			11	y	y	y	y	27	y	G	y	G	43 end size 4 & 6
G	G	G	G	12	y	y	y	y	28	y	t	y	t	44
G	G	G	G	13	y	y	y	y	29	g	t	g	t	45
t	G	t	G	14	t	t	y	y	30	t	t	t	t	46
G	t	G	t	15	t	t	y	y	31	t	t	G	G	47
t	G	t	G	16	y	g	y	g	32	t	t	G	G	48 end size 8 & 10

Cuff color chart

G	G	t	t	1
G	G	t	t	2
G	G	G	G	3
G	G	G	G	4
t	g	t	g	5
g	t	g	t	6
y	y	y	y	7

Rapunzel
Let down your cables

Named because of the flowing cables from the neck, this cabled pullover is knit from the neck down with sport weight or dk weight yarn. Increases are hidden with the cables for a smooth layout.

Sizes
Child's sizes: **1, 2, 4, 6.** Instructions are written for smallest size with larger sizes in parenthesis.

Sweater pictured knit with Paton's True North dk yarn

Finished Chest Measurements
Chest circumference: 21 (24, 27, 30)"

Materials
Yarn Dk weight total yardage needed: 450 (500, 600, 700) yds
Circular Needles One pair each size 4 and 6 16" length
Double Point Needles Size 4 and 6.
Cable Needle
Tapestry Needle

Gauge
5 to 6 st and 7 to 8 rows = 1" Knit with size 6 needles and sport weight yarn in Stockinette St. Gauge will vary with different yarns.

Neck Ribbing

With size 4 circular 16" needles CO 84 (84, 96, 96) sts, turn.

K3 (3, 4, 4), p4; rep between *'s to beginning. Turn.

Row 1: P3 (3, 4, 4), k4; rep around, join beg to end, make sure stitches are not twisted. Place marker after first 2 purl sts are worked on next row. Continue slipping marker even though the beginning of row will be 2 sts in front of it.

Rows 2 to 5: P3 (3, 4, 4), k4; rep around.

Row 6: * P3 (3, 4, 4), knit 4 stitch left cable (sl 2 sts to cable needle (cn), hold in front, k2, k2 sts from cn.) * rep bet *'s to beginning marker.

Rep rows 1 to 6: 1 (1, 2, 2) more times for a total of 2 (2, 3, 3) cables twists. Work rows 2 to 5 one more time.

Yoke

Change to larger size 6 16" circular needles.

Row 1: (Cable twist row): P1 inc ,*4 st lt cable, p1inc in first p st after cable. P1 (1, 2, 2), P1inc in p st before cable,* repeat between *'s.

Row 2: Purl p sts, knit k sts including the inc st on each side of the cable, cable will now be a 6 st cable. Always knit 6 cable sts as established, p inc sts between cables as they are added on increase rows. This number will increase as cable twists are added every 5 rows.

Rows 3, 4, 5, 6: Knit k sts, and purl p sts.

Row 7: (Inc row and Cable row) *Work p1inc on last p st before cable, twist cable and inc 1 st in first st after cable. Repeat rows 3 to 7 increasing on cable row until yoke measures: 6 (7, 8, 9)".

Sleeves

From beginning marker, knit past 2 cables plus 2 sts. Change to size 6 dp needles and divide sts evenly while knitting. This next section will be the sleeve. Knit past 2 cables and to within 2 sts of the next cable. Place marker at center of arm inseam and join sleeve to knit circular.

Sleeve decrease

Knit sleeves circular working rows 3 to 7. After 3 cables are completed, begin sleeve decreases by k2tog before and after marker at inseam. Continue dec 1 sts on each side of the marker on every row you twist the cable. When sleeve measures 6 (7, 9, 11)" from underarm inseam making sure you have a multiple of 7 sts. Change to smaller size 4 needles.

Cuff

K4, p3, sts may need to be decreased to have a multiple of 7. Work to marker. Continue twisting k4 with 4 st left cable every 4th row. Slip sts over to other sleeve section making sure you have the same number of sts on front and back.   Repeat for other sleeve:

Body

There will be 4 cables down front plus the 2 purl sts on each side these remaining sts are the body. When joining the front and back, you can pick up 2 to 3 sts under each arm from the sleeve to close the gap. On the next round, you can k2tog two times to decrease the sts added to close gap. Continue with est cable pattern. There will only be 4 purl sts between side cables when joining. Continue established cable and purl pattern for 6 (7, 9, 11)", Change to smaller size 4 needles.

Bottom Cuff

K4, p3 around for first round. Try to line up the k4 in the middle of the established 6 cable sts so they flow into the ribbing. A few sts may need to be decreased to accomplish this as you knit around on first row of ribbing. Purl p sts and knit k sts for 3 more rounds, then work 4 st lt cable twists on k4 sts. Work 3 more cable twists every 4th row. Work 2 more rows of k4, p3.
Bind off loosely.

Finishing

With contrasting color and tapestry needle, embroider 3 small 5 petal flowers down the front middle after the ribbing. The petals are a chain st worked in a circle with a french knot in the center. Two green leafs are embroidered on each flower.

Embroidered flowers

Finished sweater measurements

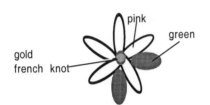

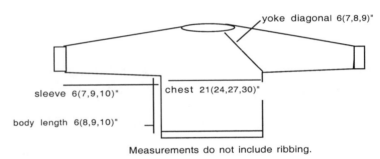

Measurements do not include ribbing.

Strawberry Twist

Looks yummy enough to eat

This sweater is knit from the top down, the yarn overs in the yoke will make the increases smooth and flowing. The rolled edges give a relaxed finish for this colorful pullover.

Sizes
Child's sizes: **4, 6, 8, 10, 12.** Instructions are written for smallest size with larger sizes in parenthesis.

Sweater pictured knit with Patons Canadiana Colours

Finished Chest Measurements
Chest 26 (29, 33, 36, 39)"

Materials
Yarn Patons Worsted weight total yardage needed: 500 (600, 700, 950, 1100) yds.
Circular Needles One pair each circular size 4 and 8 16"length, size 8 24" length.
Double Point Needles Size 4 and 8

Gauge
4 to 5 sts and 6 to 7 rows = 1" Knit with size 8 needles with Canadiana Colours and stockinette stitch. Gauge will vary with different yarns.

Abbreviations For This Pattern

K1inc Knit into the front of the stitch and again into the back strand of the same stitch before slipping stitch off left needle.

SKP Slip 1 stitch knit wise: knit 1 st, pass slipped stitch over.

K2tog Knit 2 stitches together.

Lt tw Left twist: Will slant left, With tip of right needle, go behind first and second st on left needle, bring needle between purl wise, wrap front of 2nd st from top to bottom around right needle and pull through to back wrap yarn and bring st forward knit wise, then, knit first st on left needle, drop both sts off left needle at same time

Rt tw Right twist: will slant right, with right needle, knit second stitch first, then first st, by slipping rt needle knit wise, through second stitch, wrap st and bring forward as knit st, don't drop st off, then knit first st and drop both off at the same time. From before a twist st to after a twist st is one "section". You will count sections later on to divide for sleeves, front and back.

Note Photocopy pattern and check off each row as it is knit to help keep track of place.

Neck

With size 4 needles, cast on 80 (80, 96, 96, 96) sts.

Join to knit circular making sure stitches are not twisted. Place beginning marker.

Rolled edge: Knit 6 rounds slipping beg marker each round.

Row 1: K2, p2; rep around to beg marker.

Rep row 1 lining up knit and purl sts for 1 1/2".

Change to larger size 8 16" needles. (When more stitches are added to yoke, change to 24" length so 16" can be used for sleeves.) Smaller sizes may use dp for entire sleeve and cuff.

___**Row 1:** *Rt tw, k1, m1, k1;* (Rep each row between *'s around to beginning marker.)

___**Row 2:** *Lt tw, k3,*

___**Row 3**: *Rt tw, k1, yo, skp,*

___**Row 4:** *Lt tw , k3,*

___**Row 5:** *Rt tw, k 3,*

___**Row 6:** *Lt tw, yo, k1, k2tog, yo,* (inc row)

___**Row 7:** *Rt tw, k4,* (you may have to move marker 1 place)

___**Row 8:** *Lt tw, k4,*

___**Row 9:** *Rt tw, yo, k2tog, k2tog, yo,*

___**Row 10:** *Lt tw, k4,*

___**Row 11:** *Rt tw, k1, yo, k1, yo, skp,*

___**Row 12:** *Lt tw, k5,*

___**Row 13:** *Rt tw, k5,*

___**Row 14:** *Rt tw, k2tog, yo, k1inc, yo, skp,* (inc row)

___**Row 15:** *Lt tw, k6,*

___**Row 16:** *Rt tw, k2tog, yo, k2, yo, skp,*

___**Row 17:** *Lt tw, k6,*

___**Row 18:** *Rt tw, k6,*

___**Row 19:** *Lt tw, k2tog, yo, k1, m1, k1, yo, skp,* (inc row)

___**Row 20:** *Rt tw, k7,*

___**Row 21:** *Lt tw, k2tog, yo, k3, yo, skp,*

___**Row 22:** *Rt tw, k7,*

___**Row 23:** *Lt tw, k7,*

___**Row 24:** *Rt tw, k2tog, yo, k1, m1, k2, yo, skp,* (inc row)

___**Row 25:** *Lt tw, k8,*

___**Row 26:** *Rt tw, k2tog, yo, k4, yo, skp,*

___**Row 27:** *Lt tw, k8,*

___**Row 28:** *Rt tw, k2tog, yo, k4, yo, skp,*

___**Row 29:** *Lt tw, k8,*

End here for size 4 Yoke should measure from base of neck ribbing to end approx 7" 20 sections of 10 sts 200 sts

Size 6:

___**Row 30:** *Rt tw, k2tog, yo, k2, yo, k2, yo, skp,* (inc row)

___**Row 31:** *Lt tw, k9,*

___**Row 32:** *Rt tw, k2tog, yo, k2tog, yo, k1, yo, skp, yo, skp,*

___**Row 33:** *Lt tw, k9,*

___**Row 34:** *Rt tw, k2tog, yo, k2tog, yo, k1, yo, skp, yo, skp,*

___**Row 35:** *Lt tw, k9,*

End here for size 6 Yoke should measure from base of neck ribbing to end approx 8" 20 sections of 11 sts, 220 sts.

Size 8:

___**Row 36:** *Rt tw, k2tog, yo, k2tog, yo, k1inc, yo, skp, yo, skp,* (inc row)

___**Row 37:** *Lt tw, k10,*

___**Row 38:** *Rt tw, k2tog, yo, k2tog, yo, k2, yo, skp, yo, skp,*

___**Row 39:** *Lt tw, k10,*

___**Row 40:** *Rt tw, k2tog, yo, k2tog, yo, k2, yo, skp, yo, skp,*

___**Row 41:** *Lt tw, k10,*

End here for size 8 Yoke should measure from base of neck ribbing to end approx 9" 24 sections of 12 sts, 288 sts.

Size 10:

___**Row 42:** *Rt tw, k2tog, yo, k2tog, yo, k1, yo, k1, yo, skp, yo, skp,* (inc row)

___**Row 43:** *Lt tw, k11,*

___**Row 44:** *Rt tw, k2tog, yo, k2tog, yo, k3, yo, skp, yo, skp,*

___**Row 45:** *Lt tw, k11,*

___**Row 46:** *Rt tw, k2tog, yo, k2tog, yo, k3, yo, skp, yo, skp,*

___**Row 47:** *Lt tw, k11,*

End here for size 10: Yoke should measure from base of neck ribbing to end approx 10" 24 sections of 13 sts, 312 sts.

Size 12:

___**Row 48:** *Rt tw, k2tog, yo, k2tog, yo, k2, yo, k2, yo, skp, yo, skp,* (inc row)

___**Row 49:** *Lt tw, k12,*

___**Row 50:** *Rt tw, k2tog, yo, k2tog, yo,k5, yo, skp, yo, skp,*

___**Row 51:** *Lt tw, k12,*

___**Row 52:** *Rt tw, k2tog, yo, k2tog, yo, k5, yo, skp, yo, skp,*

___**Row 53:** *Lt tw, k12,*

End here for size 12:

Yoke should measure from base of neck ribbing to end approx 11" 24 sections of 14 sts, 336 sts total.

Sleeve

Keeping all other sts on needles, use the 16" length size 8 needles or size 8 dp needles and knit over sleeve section. Beg marker should be in front of a twist st. Work last two rows of yoke pattern, not including an increase row, over 5 (5, 6, 6, 6) sections or 50 (55, 72, 78, 84) sts. Join and placing marker to knit sleeve circular. Cont pattern for sleeve by repeating last 2 rows that were knit for yoke. Decrease two sts by k2tog every 6th row before and after marker. Two sts will be decreased every 6th row. Knit sleeve until inseam measures 7 (9, 10, 11, 12, 13)"

Cuff

Change to size 4 circular needles, k2, p2, ribbing for 1 1/2". Knit 6 rows for curled edge, bind off loosely. Slip sts over 5 (5, 6, 6, 6) sections and repeat for other sleeve, make sure front and back match in number of sts.

Body

All remaining sts are body of sweater. Attach yarn and join front and back to knit body circular. Pattern should continue working last two rows of yoke, as was done for sleeves.

Note There will be a small hole under each sleeve where front and back are joined. This gap can be knit closed or sewn later after sweater is completed.

Sewing method After sweater is completed, use a tapestry needle and yarn and whip stitch the gap closed. Knit body in est pattern until it measures the desired length, or the length of the sleeves, 7 (8, 9, 10, 11)".

Finished sweater measurements

Body Ribbing

Change to smaller size 4 needles and work k2, p2 ribbing for 1 1/2". K 6 rows then bind off loosely and weave in ends.

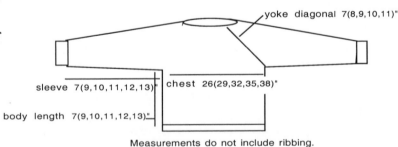

Measurements do not include ribbing.

58

Design Challenge

Create your own memory sweater. The sweater pictured was knit for my father with his hobbies and interests as the topic for motifs. I graphed on paper a small picture of what he liked, then colored it on graph paper. I tried to limit the colors used at one time to 2 or 3 colors. For some of the motifs, I alternated them upside down, right side up for a unique look. I worked the increases every other row in between the designs. If you look closely, you can see his name, and many of his hobbies which include, music, saxophone, ceramics, medicine, pottery, bowling, fish and it buttoned with coin buttons. Lots of fun and really not too hard, just exciting to see the sweater come to life.

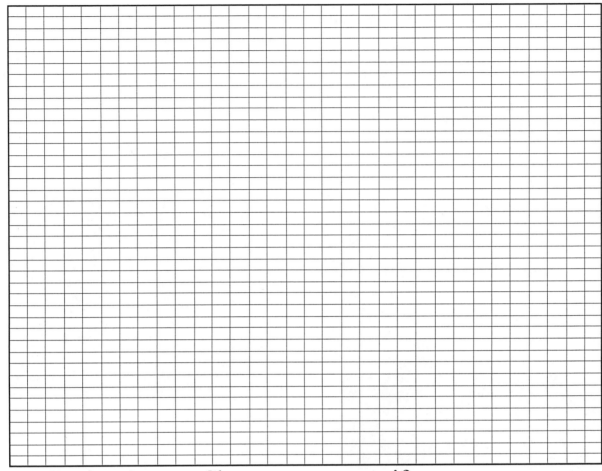

Design Away....Chart your own motifs.

Suggested Yarn Sources

Heindselmans Knit Shop
176 West Center Street
Provo, Utah
801-373-5193 fax 801 373-9664

The Knitting room
3189 Meridian Ave
San Jose CA 95124
408 264-7229
Knitroom@aol.com

Lion Brand Yarn CO
34 West 15 Street
New York, NY 10011
800-258-9276

www.the-mannings.com

www.wanderings.com

Needles'n Pins Yarn Shoppe
W9034 County Trunk A
Delavan WI 53115
www.needlespinsyarnshoppe.com

Patternworks Yarn Warehouse
Poughkeepsie, NY
1-800-438-5464
www.patternworks.com
knit@patternworks.com

Plymouth Yarn Co., Inc
P.O. Box 28
Bristol, PA 19007
http://www.plymouthyarn.com

Unique One
P.O. Box 744
Camden ME 04843
www.mainesweaters.com

**Wanderknits-Country Store & Mail
    Order**
1944 Washington Valley Rd.
Martinsville, NJ 08836
800 456-knit www.elan.com

Weaver's Loft
Yarnshop@aol.com
800 693-7243

YarnXpress
www.YarnXpress.com
info@yarnxpress.com
23 Compass Avenue
West Milford, NY 07480

Stitch Glossary

Approx: An abbreviation for the word approximately.

Bind off (bo) Decreasing stitches at end of work to finish off edge.

Cast on (co) Adding stitches to the needles to knit.

Contrasting color (cc) Colors in the work that are used less than the others.

Chain (ch) An abbreviation for a crocheted chain stitch made by making a loop and drawing the yarn through the loop with the crochet hook.

Color Chart Chart that is followed for color changes in garment. Start chart from the bottom right side on row 1 and start each row from the right side unless otherwise noted.

Continue (cont) Keep working as you have been.

Decrease (dec) A process to take away sts so there are fewer than originally.

Double Point (dp) Needles that are pointed on both ends, used to knit circular.

Duplicate stitch An embroidery stitch worked on top of the knitting, woven to look like a knit stitch.

Established (est) An abbreviation for established.

Fair Isle A combination of different colors worked together in a design, usually.

Garter Stitch A type of knitting in which the knit stitch is worked on both sides, leaving a ridge for each row.

Gauge The number of stitches and row in a knitted sample.

Increase (inc) You will increase a stitch either by M1 or K1inc where indicated in pattern.

Garter Stitch Both sides of the work are knit. Knit on the knit side of the work and knit on the purl side also.

Knit (k) Abbreviation for knit.

Knit in front and back A method of increasing one stitch by knitting into the front of the stitch and before dropping it off the needle, knitting into the back of the same stitch.

Knit Two Stitches Together (K2tog) Knit 2 stitches together. Place needle through second and first stitch at the same time, follow through with the knit stitch.

Knit One Stitch and Increase (K1inc) Knit into the front of the stitch and into knit normally and before slipping stitch off needle, knit again into the back strand of the same stitch, then slip stitch off left needle.

Knitwise Insert the needle front to back as if to knit.

Left Cable (lt cable) Placing sts on a cable needle and holding to the front of the work, the next sts are worked, then the sts from the cable needle are worked for a twisted appearance.

Left Twist (Lt tw)= Left twist-Will slant left, With tip of right needle, go behind first and second st on left needle, bring needle between purl wise, wrap front of 2nd st from top to bottom around right needle and pull through to back wrap yarn and bring st forward knit wise, then, knit first st on left needle, drop both sts off left needle at same time

Marker (m) A small ring or other item used to mark place on needle.

Main Color (mc) The color of yarn used most in the knitting.

Make One Stitch (M1) With left needle tip, lift the strand between the last knitted stitch and the first stitch on the left needle, from front to back, knit through the back of the lifted strand, this will not leave a hole.

Multiple The number of stitches that make up a sequence of stitces that are in a pattern.

Parenthesis Curved vertical lines that contain directions that will be repeated.

Pass Slipped Stitch Over (psso) After

slipping a stitch from the left needle to the right, the instructions may have "psso." You work the next stitch after slipping a stitch, then slip the left needle through the slipped stitch and lift it over the last stitch worked. This will decrease 1 stitch.

Picot A series of bumps along a knitted edge.

Purl (p) Work the next stitch a purl. Slip the needle from back to front and from the top down.

Purlwise Insert the needle from the back to the front as you would to purl.

Raglan sleeve A type of sleeve that tapers from the neck down to the arm on a diagonal.

repeat (rep) Means to do something over again.

Ribbing A name for fabric that is worked in such a way that gives it elasticity, usually a combination on knit and purl stitches.

Round In circular knitting, each row is sometimes called a round.

Right Hand (rh) Reference to right hand, stitches or needle.

Right Side (RS) Refers to the right side of the work.

Right Cable (rt cable) Placing sts on a cable needle and holding to the back of the work, the next sts are worked, then the sts from the cable needle are worked for a twisted appearance.

Right Twist (rt tw) Right twist will slant right, with right needle, knit second stitch first, then first st, by slipping rt needle knit wise, through second stitch, wrap st and bring forward as knit st, don't drop st off, then knit first st and drop both off at the same time.

Short row A way of turning part way through a row and working back and forth over stitches to create extra rows for a more comfortable shaping,.

Slip,Knit, Pass Slipped Stitch over Knit Stitch (skp) Slip one stitch from left needle to right needle, work the next stitch, then pass slipped stitch over the kit stitch.

Slip stitch (sl 1) Slip a stitch from the left needle to the right needle. Place the right needle through the loop on the left needle as if you were purling. Slip it over to the other needle without working it. Slip stitch is done.

Slip Marker (sm) Slip marker from the left needle to the right needle.

Stockinette Stitch (St st) If knitting circular, you will knit all rows circular. If working two sided, you will knit the right side and purl the wrong side.

Through Back Loop (tbl) Instead of knitting into the front of the stitch, place needle through the back loop instead and work the stitch as usual.

Work Refers to the project you are working on.

WS Abbreviation for the wrong side.

Yarn Back (yb) Place throw yarn to the back of the work as if to knit.

Yarn Forward (yf) Place throw yarn to the front of the work as if to purl.

Yarn Over (yo) Place throw yarn to the opposite direction, up and over work to the other side.

Yards (yds) Measurement of yarn.

Index

a
abbreviations 3
adding colors 8
aran knits 5
Around & About 16
b
binding off 11, 59
-picot edge 11
blocking 11
bulky yarn 6
buttonbands 11
-garter 11
-ribbing 11
buttonholes 10
Button up pattern 24
c
casting on 7, 59
 -thumb wrap cast on 7
circular needles 6
colors, adding 8
contrasting color 59
Country Checked cardigan 44
d
design challenge 57
double point needles 6
duplicate stitch 59
e
embroidery 44
f
fair isle 17, 59
flowered cables pattern 40
g
garter stitch 59
gauge 5, 6, 59
h
hood 23
I
increase stitch 7, 59
j
just peachy pattern 28
k
k1inc 8
knit' n hood pattern 20
knit 2 together 59
knitting the waves pattern 36
l
left cable 59
left twist 59
length 11

m
Make one 7, 59
-scattering 8
markers 8
-commercial markers 9
-M1 and fair isle 8
metric 5
mock turtleneck 13
motifs 8
n
needles 6
needle conversion chart 5
non mercerized cotton 4
notes on patterns 3
p
patterns, reading 7
picot edge 33, 60
plain & simple pattern 12
psso 60
pullover to cardigan 11
purlwise 60
r
raglan sleeve 60
raglanless to raglan 8
ribbing 9
right cable 60
right twist 60
Ripple Knits'kin pattern 32
rolled edge 9
s
Shades of Gray pattern 53
short rows 9, 10, 60
-directions 10
-explanation 9
sizing 9
skp 60
sleeve decrease 60
sleeves, knitting flat 10
slip stitch 60
stickies 9
stitch glossary 50-60
stripeless stripe 8
stockinette stitch 60
t
Teaching others to knit 61
through back loop 60
Twist'n Knit pattern 48
u
under arm gap 10

w
worsted weight yarn 6
wrong side 60
y
yardage chart 4
yards 60
yarn 4
-amount 4
-colors 4
-fiber content 4
-texture 4
-weight 4
-yardage needed 5
yarn back 60
yarn forward 60
yarn gauge 4
yarn over 60
yarn sources 58
yoke 8

About Mary Rich Goodwin

Knitting became Mary's passion at age eight when her grandmother taught her to knit. By age twelve, she was knitting sweaters for family and friends. Her oldest sister, a beautiful knitter born with only one arm and with two small fingers on her right shoulder, taught her new techniques and encouraged her. Her oldest brother, during the VietNam War, learned to knit warm sweaters for himself and others while stationed at a post where he had months of solitude. Her parents, both artists, encouraged her to develop artistic talent in whatever area she worked. They always found the good in her work and a compliment was always waiting.

Mary obtained her teaching degree in Health Education in 1980 from BYU, a Masters Degree in Education in 1988 from Weber State University, and a Masters Degree in Educational Leadership in 1994 from BYU. She has taught Junior High for 19 years, and has written curriculum for her school district. She married in 1980.

Her six children, including five boys and one girl, have been the inspiration for many of her designs. When they were young, money was tight and knitting sweaters was not only fun, but economical. Mary explains that her life has been extremely busy and hectic and she firmly believes that knitting is an excellent form of therapy since it engages one's hands and produces an outcome that brings great satisfaction to oneself and to others.

She is also an advocate for and has participated in humanitarian efforts throughout the world. As a result of donated knitting projects, leapers have comfortable knitted and crocheted bandages, premature babies have caps, and many babies have afghans and booties. Mary encourages others to become involved, saying that there is nothing more satisfying than to give a nice handmade gift to someone and know that you are giving it from your heart.

Mary welcomes comments from her readers and fellow knitters. She encourages people to submit their own designs to knitting magazines.